Praise for
UNCOVERING *The* LOGIC *of* ENGLISH

Awards received:

Silver Medalist - Independent Publisher Book Awards 2011

Gold Medalist - Indie Excellence Awards

Finalist - ForeWord Reviews

Winner - Midwest Book Awards

Finalist - Benjamin Franklin Awards 2012

"A clarion call to all teachers of reading. This book is a must read for anyone who cares about the future of our children and the welfare of our nation."

—*Dr. Robert W. Sweet, Jr,* President
The National Right to Read Foundation

"A gem of a book that brings light to the way in which words are read and spelled. This is a very useful book for teachers, parents and anyone interested in bringing the joy of reading to our nation's children."

—*Dr. Reid Lyon,* Distinguished Professor of Education Policy,
Southern Methodist University

"*Uncovering the Logic of English* is a thoughtful guide for anyone who wants to understand language better or is looking for advice to help them teach it."

—*Midwest Book Review*

"It looks fabulous—like a resource I've been looking for for about 15 years!"

—*Speech Therapist*

"The 'thrust' of this book might be better described if the title was changed to *The Heartbreak of English: a Logical Means of Recovery.*"

—*Jack Blackburn,* Retired 3M Engineer

"The best spelling and reading book ever!"

—*Teacher*

"A must-read for anyone involved in teaching literacy."

—*Cathie Baier,* Homeschool Speaker and Parent

"This book is changing my life. If you struggle with reading, or know anyone that does, *Uncovering the Logic of English* is totally worth it!"

—*Allie Gower,* Designer

"I teach language arts to middle school students with autism. My literal, logical thinking students are frustrated daily by the seemingly endless exceptions to the rules of the English language. Until today, the only answer I ever had for them was, 'The English language is full of exceptions to the rules. Be glad you are learning it as your native language and have had the benefit of years of immersion.' This is of little comfort to them. I finally have a comprehensive list of the real rules of the English language! The best thing of all is that experts talk a lot about using the obsessions of students with autism to teach them. Most of my students are obsessed with rules (memorizing them, following them to the very literal letter, and making sure others follow them as well), so I am confident that they will enthusiastically devour and retain this information! For the first time since learning to diagram sentences in college, when parts of speech rules really clicked for me, I am excited to teach English!"

—*Jenny Lundgren,* Middle School Teacher

"Denise Eide's book is outstanding! I could not put it down when I started reading it. Wish all schools could use it as a text."

—*Sharon Campbell,* parent and grandmother

"Once it is understandably explained to you, the perceived illogical spelling system of the English language actually starts to make a lot of sense—and FUN! My first language is German—completely different spelling system—and I learned to read and write in English 'the old way'. It did work alright, but I know, had I been taught the way described in *Uncovering the Logic of English*, it would have been SO much easier!"

—*Valerie Adomakoh,* parent, non-native English speaker

"I am a certified reading specialist and have been studying reading instruction for years, but most of the information in Eide's book was completely new to me... If you are a parent or educator, this passage from Eide's is a MUST-READ! She provides critical information and insights for all of us..."

—*Susan Kruger, M.Ed.,* author of the best-selling book *SOAR Study Skills* and founder of www.StudySkills.com

UNCOVERING
The LOGIC *of*
ENGLISH

A Common-Sense Approach to Reading, Spelling, and Literacy

DENISE EIDE

PEDIALEARNING
INCORPORATED

Uncovering the Logic of English: A Common-Sense Approach to Reading, Spelling, and Literacy

Copyright © 2011, 2012 Pedia Learning Inc.

Pedia Learning Inc.
10800 Lyndale Ave S. Suite 181
Minneapolis, MN 55420
United States of America

Previously published as *Uncovering the Logic of English: A Common-Sense Solution to America's Literacy Crisis,* © 2011

Cover design: Dugan Design Group
Interior design and typsetting: Katherine Lloyd, The Desk
Printed in the United States of America

ISBN 978-1-936706-21-1

Library of Congress Control Number: 2012941978

Second edition paperback
10 9 8 7 6 5 4 3 2

This book is dedicated to all students of English.
I hope it brings clarity where there was confusion
and renews hope for those who have struggled.

ACKNOWLEDGMENTS

Many thanks to everyone who has contributed to this work! It would not have been possible without you. Thank you to Nathan Eide, Timothy Eide, Sara Eppinga, Jamie Calvert, Kristi Bakken, Amy Conners, and Martine Haglund who encouraged me to begin this project and encouraged me along the way.

Thank you to Carmita Sequeira, Kimber Iverson, Kristi Laidlaw, Jean Deming, Martine Haglund, Valerie Kiger, Nathan Eide, Timothy Eide, Beverly Eide, Valerie Adomakoh, Pavel Romaniko, Jenny Reichmann, Paul Hawley, and everyone who has provided editing and feedback. Your questions, comments, encouragement and critique have added clarity and power to the book. You have challenged me to research and dig deeper, making this a more usable and readable book for everyone.

My deepest gratitude is to my family for believing in me, encouraging me, giving me space to write and rewrite and rewrite, reading drafts, and running our home and business. You have been unbelievably supportive. Thank you so much: Nathan, Miriam, Abraham, Josiah, Hannah, Tim, Bev, Vernon, Kimber, and Andy for helping me fulfill a dream.

Soli Deo Gloria

CONTENTS

Introduction *11*

1. The Problem of English. 15

2. The Literacy Crisis. 21

3. Phonograms: The Building Blocks of Words 25

4. Consonants, Vowels, and Syllables: What They Are
   and Why They Matter 37

5. Foundational Consonant Rules 41

6. Foundational Vowel Rules. 49

7. The Mystery of Silent Final E's Solved! 63

8. Words Ending in One Vowel and One Consonant. 77

9. Adding Suffixes to Single Vowel Y Words 87

10. Adding Suffixes to Any Word 91

11. The Power of the Latin Spellings of /sh/ 95

12. Decoding Past Tense Verbs. 101

13. Forming Plural Nouns and Singular Verbs. 107

14. Clearing Confusion about al- and -ful 113

15. The Final Spelling Rules 115

16. Overcoming Challenges: Creating an Auditory Picture 121

17. Efficient Spelling and Vocabulary Development 129

18. Putting It All Together 141

Appendix A: Spelling Rules................................. 151

Appendix B: Basic Phonograms 153

Appendix C: More about the Basic Phonograms 157

Appendix D: Sound to Spelling Reference..................... 167

Appendix E: Advanced Phonograms 169

Appendix F: Adding a Suffix to Any Word.................... 171

Appendix G: Irregular Verbs................................ 173

Appendix H: Irregular Plurals 179

Appendix I: Common Prefixes and Suffixes................... 183

Appendix J: American, British, Canadian & Australian Spellings ... 185

Resources.. 193

Glossary.. 195

Bibliography 197

Notes 199

Subject Index.. 201

TABLES

Table 1: Single-Letter Phonograms 29

Table 2: Multi-Letter Phonogram Sounds 32-33

Table 3: Multi-Letter Phonogram Spelling Aids 34-35

Table 4: Single-Letter Vowels 50

Table 5: Multi-Letter Vowels 50-51

Table 6: Foreign Words Ending in I 55

Table 7: Foreign Words Ending in U 55

Table 8: Slang Words Ending in I and U 56

Table 9: Suffixes Used with the Latin Spellings 96

Table 10: Latin Roots Using TI 97

Table 11: Latin Roots Using CI 97

Table 12: Latin Roots Using SI 97

Table 13: Latin Roots Using the Voiced Sound of SI 98

Table 14: Base Words Ending in BB 119

Table 15: Base Words Ending in DD. 119

Table 16: Base Words Ending in GG. 119

Table 17: Base Words Ending in NN. 119

Table 18: Base Words Ending in RR 119

Table 19: Base Words Ending in TT 119

Table 20: Base Words Ending in ZZ 119

Table 21: Twenty Most Frequently Used Words. 129

Table 22: 9 Most Common Prefixes 133

Table 23: 10 Most Common Suffixes. 134

INTRODUCTION

A s I have spoken with people around the country, I have discovered a pervasive belief: English spelling is inconsistent, illogical, and, for some, impossible. This apparent "flaw" with English has caused deep frustration not only within our schools—public, private, and home—but through all levels of society. We have professionals who cannot spell, parents who cannot answer their children's questions, and employers who are despairing at the low literacy rates of the workforce.

Language, both spoken and written, is the foundation of all academics and the medium by which we conduct business, science, politics, and relationships. Without a firm grasp of our language, we sever the Achilles tendon of our society and of the individuals within it.

The United States currently has one of the lowest literacy rates in the developed world. According to the Nation's Report Card, 34% of fourth graders cannot read, and 68% are below proficient.[1] An astounding 68% of eighth graders test below grade level in reading.[2] These statistics continue on through the adult population; fully 48% of adults are not proficient in reading.[3]

This is at a time in history when the economy demands more highly skilled workers each year, and competition in highly trained fields such as science and engineering is exploding worldwide. Not only do we need to increase literacy rates to stay competitive in a world economy, but illiteracy and remedial education cost our nation $536 billion each year[4] and are primary factors in both crime and poverty.[5] Teaching reading so that everyone succeeds is vital to the health of our society and our economy.

The information contained in *Uncovering the Logic of English* is not new. You may be surprised to learn that, with some variations, the spelling rules and phonograms already are used with great success by dyslexia institutes and reading centers around our nation. For unknown reasons, this "intensive phonics" is saved almost exclusively for students who struggle. I simply cannot understand why material that effectively teaches almost all students[6] has been reserved for remedial reading centers. As a nation, we need to rethink how reading is taught in our schools and thereby prevent many children from needing outside help in the first place.

As you read, I hope it becomes apparent that knowing the logic of English benefits everyone who uses this language. You, too, might shake your head at points in this book and say, "Why didn't someone tell me this before?" In these pages, you will discover the answers to your long-held questions about English, and you will learn answers for your children as they are learning to read and spell.

I have taught numerous reading and spelling classes ranging from 45 minutes to three days in length. The participants have included teachers from public and private schools, special education teachers, and homeschool parents. The response has been unanimous: "Why wasn't I taught this in elementary school? It all makes so much sense!" Many professional teachers have told me after a one-hour presentation, "I learned more in one hour than in all my methods classes in graduate school."

With this information I am resoundingly confident that we can teach reading at a fraction of the cost, and with much higher success rates, than we currently do. To do so, it is essential that all students, all teachers, and all parents know the logic of English. The knowledge in this book is as basic to academic success as $1 + 1 = 2$.

Learning these basic concepts does not require expensive materials or a lot of resources. It simply requires teachers who know how English works and how students learn. When we combine the logic of English with strong methods, our whole society will reap the rewards economically, scientifically, educationally, and politically. Imagine a nation where 99% of third graders read at or above grade level and where our high schools are dominated not by students who are discouraged and frustrated but by confident young adults who are preparing to fulfill their life mission.

Although I understand that, to some, reading a book of English rules might sound dull, I encourage you to let this book unfold the mystery of what may have seemed hopelessly chaotic. It will provide you with information you will be able to apply as soon as you sit down to write your next e-mail. You may also experience, as I do, that the coherence in the midst of complexity is more alluring than if it had been in plain sight all along.

I hope you find this information as engaging and enlightening as I have and that you pass this book on to many others so that everyone can begin to understand the logic of English.

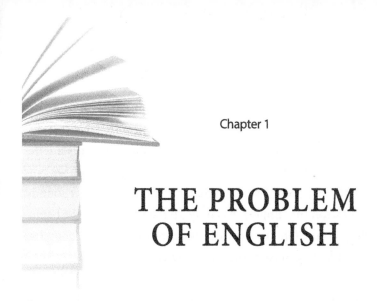

Chapter 1

THE PROBLEM
OF ENGLISH

A t the level of the written word, English is one of the most complex languages in the world. Due to this complexity, most English speakers do not know the basic building blocks of the language: the sounds, their corresponding written expressions, and the spelling rules that go with them.

On the contrary, most English speakers are cynical about the language and readily dismiss it as a language of exceptions. But what if the problem is not the language itself but the rules we were taught? What if we could see the complexity of English as a powerful tool rather than a hindrance?

Certainly, it is not as easy to learn to read and spell English as it is most other phonetic languages. Yet a finite number of tools unlock the mystery of 98% of the words in the English language. When these 105 tools are presented, nearly all students can succeed.

Learning these tools also develops logic and higher-order thinking skills. When students learn to think systematically about English, a complex language, not only do they enhance their English language skills, but they also gain strategies by which to master foreign languages.

To begin, we must understand the definition of **word**. Spoken words in all languages are formed by combining one or more sounds. This series of sounds carries meaning. Each sound is called a **phoneme**. English is comprised of 44 unique phonemes which combine together to form words.

This presents the first problem: the 26 letters of the Latin alphabet are inadequate to describe the 44 spoken phonemes or sounds. To solve this discrepancy, English adds 48 multi-letter phonograms. A **phonogram** is a letter or combination of letters which represents one or more sounds. When we only teach children the alphabet, even if we include long and short vowel sounds, we give the false impression that English has only 31 sounds. This is the beginning of the prevailing confusion. To provide students with a more complete understanding of English they must master not only 26 letters but the 74 basic phonograms.

The second problem with English is that the language contains immense variety and choice. The 44 sounds can be spelled in 74 basic ways, 25 of which make more than one sound. The fact that phonograms frequently say more than one sound results from the fact English words often shift in pronunciation when suffixes and prefixes are added. Consider the sounds of the A in *vacate, evacuate,* and *vacation.* In order to preserve the relationship in meaning between each of these words, the A represents three different sounds. Due to the unique challenges with spoken English, spellings are chosen to represent sound while preserving meaning. In other words, English is a morpho-phonemic language where the morphology or meaning of words is balanced with the phonemic representation of words, resulting in some phonograms representing multiple sounds. This means a student of English must learn all the sounds represented by each phonogram.

The third problem is that phonograms alone do not unlock the mystery of English spelling. There are 31 spelling rules which interplay with the phonograms and affect the pronunciation and spelling of words. These rules apply to a vast majority of words and explain why they are spelled and pronounced in a particular manner. Without an understanding of these simple rules, some scholars have estimated English to have over 1,700 phonograms![1] The 31 rules that explain how the sounds interplay with one another bring order to the chaos.

The fourth problem is that English is an amalgamation of languages. England's location and history of occupation play a significant role in the development of modern-day English. It is beyond the scope of this book to describe the history of this development, but a few of the highlights are pertinent to our topic. From AD 43 to 410 the British Isles were occupied by Rome. This brought about a heavy influence of Latin. In fact, 90% of multisyllable words in English have Latin roots.[2]

After the Norman Invasion in 1066, the following 300 years of politics and trade were conducted in French. Many words in the English lexicon reflect this period. English is also influenced by Celtic, Norse, Anglo-Saxon, German, and increasingly other modern languages. Having grown with such rich influence, English has synonyms for most of its words, which allows for a tremendous range of meaning, precision, creativity, and expression. English is also a multi-cultural language. Words which represent objects, places, and peoples from other cultures are frequently brought into English while preserving spelling conventions from the language of origin.

This history has misled many people to believe that English no longer follows patterns, which leads to the fifth problem plaguing English—the widespread assumption that English is illogical. In reality, the logic of English has been lost in the past 80 years to educators and the general public. The keepers of this knowledge remain a few reading centers, literacy specialists, dyslexia institutes, and researchers. Experts in these fields know that a majority of children who are presented with the whole picture of English, combined with solid methods, can succeed. Nevertheless, "intensive, systematic phonics" is often taught only as a last resort to those who have the resources to hire special tutors.

It makes much more sense to provide all students with the knowledge needed to master English. After all, it is a complex code which many linguists do not understand. Why would we abandon our young students to solve a master puzzle like English on their own?

Despite its complex phonetic system, many aspects of English are much simpler than other modern languages. English has a comparatively simple grammatical system. We do not need to memorize genders or conjugate adjectives. It has very little inflection and a comparatively short list of irregular verbs and plurals. It is helpful to remember that every language presents unique challenges to students; English is not alone. Learning to think logically about

English develops minds which are more adept at meeting the challenges of other language systems.

Learning 74 phonograms and 31 spelling rules is the most efficient route to mastering English. Put into perspective, English has the largest vocabulary in the history of the world. According to one count, there are more than 2 million words in the English lexicon.[3] The average adult speaker knows between 40,000 and 60,000 words, with a well-educated adult mastering 200,000. Surely, the most efficient way to master such a large lexicon is to learn the 105 tools which together describe each of the words.

Prior to the 1920s, reading was taught in a systematic manner, with students spelling their way into reading. A dramatic shift occurred during the educational reform movements of the 1920s and 1930s. Rather than beginning to teach reading with sounds and then using the sounds to build words, educators began with whole words. This became known as the Look-Say method. Students were required to memorize each word as an individual word picture. Today we refer to these as sight words.

During this period, literacy rates plummeted, leading to the second reform movement: Whole Language. Educators blamed illiteracy on a lack of interest due to the repetitive nature of basal readers, such as *Dick and Jane*. Whole Language educators replaced boring readers with real books. They believed learning to read was much like learning to speak. Children who were surrounded with good books would naturally develop a love for reading and, with minimal guidance, be able to read. This inspirational hands-off approach was a disaster. In California, where whole language was mandated in 1987, the functional illiteracy rate soared to 60 percent.[4]

Nevertheless, both reforms have continued to influence how we teach English reading around the world. In the 1990s, a "new eclecticism" began as educators recognized the need for phonics in the classrooms. Eclectics teach reading "progressively." They begin by teaching sight words and then progress to syllables and word families, followed by a smattering of phonics.

In addition to the inconsistent and confusing nature of the eclectic approach, it does not teach English in a complete, systematic, and logical manner. The phonics that are presented are too little, too late, and disjointed. This method dangerously gives the impression that the logic of English is being taught while leaving glaring holes in content and continuing to employ many of the failed methods of the past, including a heavy reliance on sight words.

When we teach sight words, we are effectively stripping the power of the code and asking students to memorize visual symbols for each word. Worse yet, the visual symbols have very little variation between words. How are children to memorize *bag, beg, big, bog,* and *bug* as different word pictures without knowledge of the code? They appear virtually the same. This is why so many children read the first letter and guess at the remaining word. Frequently, students taught with these methods make simple errors in reading because they are not able to handle the level of detail needed to decode the word correctly.

Diane McGuinness, PhD, has shown that human memory is limited to approximately 2,000 individual symbols.[5] Yet adult speakers of English need to master 40,000 to 200,000 words—an impossible task without the understanding of how to decipher the code. This is demonstrated by the fact that many of the adults who are functionally illiterate know between 1,000 and 2,000 sight words. Though these students were successful at the task presented to them—memorizing individual words—they are unable to use this knowledge to meaningfully decode new words and are thereby crippled from being able to read anything beyond the elementary level.

This reality is reflected by what is commonly known as The Literacy Crisis.

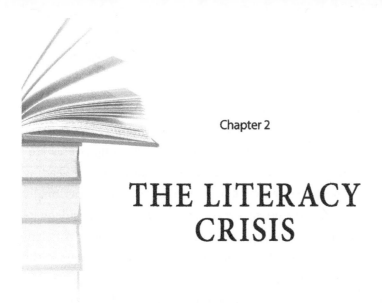

Chapter 2

THE LITERACY CRISIS

Our nation is facing a literacy crisis at all levels of the U.S. educational system. It is well-documented by the popular press, the United States government, and academia, and is felt by every teacher with whom I speak: public, private, and homeschool.

The literacy crisis resonates deeply within our hearts. For even if we were among those who learned to read proficiently, we all have unanswered questions and frustrations with English. The difference between the literate and the illiterate is that the literate blame the problems on English, but the illiterate blame themselves.

Both demonstrate misplaced blame. The problem is neither English nor individuals. The problem is that we cannot know what we were never taught.

The statistics are both numbing and consistent. Thirty-two percent of fourth graders read well, 34% test below proficiency, and 34% cannot read.[1] Every time I meet an elementary school teacher, I ask if this reflects their experience. They all say it does.

One third grade teacher who attended my class said, "This is my last resort. My principal will not allow me to teach intensive phonics in the classroom, but I am paying for my own training and using my own money to buy the kids materials. I plan to close the door and teach the children the logic of English. It makes so much sense. If it works, I will tell my administration. If it does not, I am quitting. I cannot continue failing these kids year after year."

The devastating reality is that the situation does not improve as students age. An astounding 69% of our eighth grade students are reading below grade level.[2] Twenty-six percent of eighth graders are functionally illiterate, meaning they do not possess reading and writing skills adequate to function in daily life.[3] Forty-eight percent of adults are not proficient readers, while 22% are functionally illiterate.[4] Only 3% of adults test at the highest level of reading proficiency.[5] Even when the population is limited to college graduates, the news is not encouraging. Only 10% of college graduates read at a high level of proficiency, 15% are below proficient, while 4% are functionally illiterate.[6]

The greatest complaint by employers and educators is that workers are not adequately prepared in basic reading and writing skills.[7] Their complaint reflects the reality that only 17% of working adults are both well educated and proficient in literacy skills.[8] Devastatingly, the literacy crisis is occurring during a time in history when jobs are becoming increasingly technical and the need for highly skilled workers is continually rising.

Certainly something is deeply wrong with how we are teaching reading. It is simply not conceivable that 22%–70% of our population has a reading disability. What is clear is that students who do not thrive in first, second, and third grade continue to struggle through adulthood.

It has been shown that success in reading is not linked to IQ, nor is it a problem of poverty alone. Forty-five percent of children in middle and high income families are struggling. Adult illiteracy is, however, connected to almost every socioeconomic issue in the United States.[9] Fifty percent of the chronically unemployed and 60% of inmates are illiterate.[10] Eighty-five percent of all juveniles in the court system are illiterate.[11] Low literacy levels cost between $106 and $238 billion per year in health care spending, $225 billion in nonproductivity in the workforce,[12] $1.4 billion[13] to provide remedial education for students who have recently completed high school, and $2.3[14] billion in lost earning potential.

This is a tragedy of enormous proportions to our society and to the hearts and minds of those who struggle. Yet we have known all along how to prevent the ruinous effects of illiteracy. Rudolf Flesch wrote about it in 1955 in his classic book titled *Why Johnny Can't Read*.[15] Dr. Samuel Orton performed vital research in the 1920s and '30s on reading, and scholars such as Romalda Spalding and Anna Gillingham committed their lives to preserving and developing this work. Yet on the whole, little to no improvement has been made in the past 40 years.[16]

We should all be asking, "Why?!"

Writers state that the problem stems from a variety of issues: student motivation, poverty, distractions, television, illiterate parents . . . even the recent financial crisis is blamed. The award-winning book, *Let's End Our Literacy Crisis*, claims there is one problem affecting every student: the inconsistent, illogical spelling of English words.[17] The author, Bob Cleckler, suggests that the only solution to our literacy crisis is to radically reform our spelling system.

Although it is true that children in many non–English speaking countries learn to read easily because of the one-to-one correspondence between the sounds and letters, it is not necessary to develop a new writing system for English. English already *is* phonetic. There is a solution for those who struggle with reading, and it encompasses our current spelling system. Students and their teachers and parents need to learn how English really works.

We do not need to live in crisis any longer. Researchers have demonstrated that virtually all children are able to learn to read English when taught correctly.[18] Using brain imaging technology, scientists are now able to study how our minds work while reading. People who are skilled readers rely heavily on an area of the brain which is used for speech and auditory processing and is located in the back left side of the brain. When struggling readers attempt to read, their brains show inactivity in this critical auditory region. With as little as eight weeks of intensive phonics training, the brains of struggling students begin to develop, and previously inactive areas begin to function like those of good readers.[19] Our brains are wired to learn. It is through solid phonics instruction that the brain develops pathways for reading.

When reading is not taught correctly, many students do not make solid connections between phonograms (the pictures of the sounds) and phonemes (the sounds themselves). Instead, they appear to rely heavily on the visual center of their brain and areas which may be related to higher order thinking or guessing. Given the combination of the opaque nature of the English code and teaching methods that emphasize the visual, this is not surprising. For students who are auditory or kinesthetic learners instead of visual learners, the result can be debilitating.

When the phonograms and rules of English are taught in a systematic manner through solid, multimodality teaching methods which develop visual muscle memory, prevent reversals, and address the needs of all types of learners, we will be on our way to solving the literacy crisis for all its current victims and preventing it in future generations. The logic of English needs to be taught from the very beginning of every child's education so that everyone can succeed.

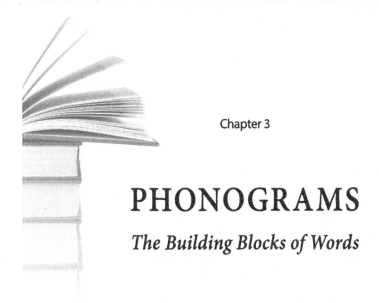

Chapter 3

PHONOGRAMS

The Building Blocks of Words

A s a society, we lack a basic grasp of English spelling. Countless highly educated professionals rely heavily on spell-checker. Yet even navigating this powerful tool can be cumbersome. Many adults need to guess multiple times before spell-checker even recognizes the word they desire to correct. Many also confess to sometimes abandoning the perfect word choice due to their inability to look it up. Knowledge of the building blocks of words, however, enables spell-checker to be used much more easily and reduces the need for it in the first place.

English is a phonetic language, albeit very complex. To teach English well, we need to move away from teaching only the names of the 26 letters and some of their sounds to teaching the true phonograms of English. **Phono** means "sound" and **gram** means "picture." A **phonogram**, therefore, is a picture that represents a sound. Phonograms may consist of one, two, three, or four letters and may represent from one to six sounds. Although most phonograms represent only one sound, a few represent a combination of two or three sounds.

Lack of knowledge about English phonograms reduces the ability to decode unfamiliar words encountered in reading. To "help" students, many schools teach "reading strategies" rather than solid phonics. Reading strategies are a series of steps students are taught to use when they encounter an unknown word. One commonly taught strategy is to look at the first and last letters of the word and then guess. Another strategy is to reread the sentence and guess from the context. A third is to look at the pictures for clues. With solid, systematic phonics education, none of these "strategies" are needed. Instead, students are provided the necessary tools to decode words internally based upon the phonograms which construct the word.

When we think of phonics, most of us think of simple examples such as "C-A-T" spells the sounds /k-ă-t/ in cat. The limited phonics we are usually taught only describes a small percentage of the language. It applies most consistently to easy, one syllable words. Most English words, however, have two or more syllables. Knowing all the phonograms and rules enables students to read a word such as *homogeneous* and understand each sound within the context of the word. (This word is explained on page 143.) When solid phonics education is combined with a foundation in the roots of words, often even the definition becomes apparent.

Phonograms are the most basic building blocks of all words in a phonetic language. Many adults in the U.S. know how to spell tens of thousands of words, but they have no idea why they are spelled in a particular manner, especially large words. Most readers rely heavily on the first and last letters of a word, with the middle of the word left as a mystery. Knowing the most basic building blocks, and being able to recognize them within words, will enable students to decode any word. This is not an innate ability but rather a skill that easily can be taught to all English speakers.

The first step is to learn the 74 basic phonograms. Phonograms can be divided into two broad categories: single-letter phonograms and multi-letter phonograms.

Single-Letter Phonograms

The single-letter phonograms are represented by the letters A–Z. These are the phonograms everyone recognizes as forming English words. Nevertheless, students are rarely taught all their sounds.

For example, consider the phonogram ⌐ s ⌐. Most programs teach that ⌐ s ⌐ has one sound, /s/. However, this does not account for very simple words such as *is, his, has, was, rise,* and *does.* When incomplete phonics is taught, students who think more logically and literally decode *is* and *his* as /ĭs/and /hĭs/ rather than /ĭz/ and /hĭz/.

It is important to understand that these students are not wrong; they are doing exactly what they were told to do.

Compounding the problem is the fact that $\boxed{s}$ is added to English nouns to form the plural. Most plurals are pronounced /z/ such as *chairs, cars, houses, tables, pencils, pens, papers,* etc. When the plurals are considered, $\boxed{s}$ says /z/ 70% of the time. Certainly a sound that occurs 70% of the time is not an exception. Both sounds should be taught clearly from the beginning.

Logical/literal students are our future engineers, mathematicians, and scientists. When we tell them that $\boxed{s}$ says /s/, they apply it to every $\boxed{s}$ they see and quickly discover that most of the S's do not say /s/. In fact, most of the letters do not sound anything like what they were told. This short-circuits their logical minds. Many of these students become discouraged by English.

I am convinced this is one of the reasons that boys tend to struggle with reading more than girls. Many boys think logically and literally. Girls generally tend to be more intuitive. Logical students do not tolerate inconsistent rules. The smattering of phonics usually given to them is not only unhelpful; it is damaging. At a time in history when our economy relies on advancements in science and engineering, we cannot afford to impair these gifted citizens by not teaching them English in a manner that respects how their minds work.

But why don't all students struggle? The sounds /s/ and /z/ are an unvoiced and voiced pair, formed in the same way in the mouth. Many intuitive students do not notice the difference between the two sounds. Their lack of concern for detail enables them to decode the words properly without complete information. These students are rewarded by today's methods. Though intuition is a great strength, their logical/literal counterparts who are attuned to detail should not be marginalized. Teaching both sounds right from the beginning allows all students to succeed and prevents student and teacher frustration by eliminating unnecessary "exceptions."

I have spoken to countless professionals who hated learning to read and write and now rely on others to proofread their written work. Yet all they needed to be successful in reading and writing was complete information. If they can learn advanced mathematics, physics, chemistry, business structures, and even other languages, they can easily learn the 105 pieces that explain English.

One final word about learning phonograms. It is important for reading and spelling to learn the phonogram sounds before the letter names. If a student learns "SEE AYE TEE," this does not tell the student how to read the word *cat*. Letter names are useful and necessary for looking up words in a dictionary, reading eye charts, reading initials in a person's name, etc. However, the letter names do not tell the student anything about how a word is read or spelled. The names are best learned after the phonogram sounds have been internalized.

Multi-Letter Phonograms

In addition to the 26 single-letter phonograms, English has 48 basic multi-letter phonograms for a total of 74. Multi-letter phonograms are fixed combinations of letters that symbolize one or more speech sounds. They may have two, three, or four letters and are called digraphs, trigraphs, and quadgraphs. It is these phonograms that are most commonly left out of incomplete phonics programs.

Many schools do teach what they believe to be phonics. They teach most of the sounds for A–Z and sometimes even a few multi-letter phonograms such as $\boxed{\text{sh}}$, $\boxed{\text{ch}}$, and $\boxed{\text{th}}$. This level of teaching often misleads students into believing that they have been given the complete picture and there is nothing left to figure out. Many students also wrongly assume that phonics must have made more sense to others. Incomplete phonics leaves a lot of holes, discouraged hearts, confused minds, and a seemingly unlimited number of exceptions.

For example, children who are not taught that $\boxed{\text{igh}}$ is "three-letter /ī/" will often carefully sound out each letter in *light* (/l-ĭ-g-h-t/) and feel utterly mystified when you suddenly announce, "That says /l-ī-t/." Simply teaching $\boxed{\text{igh}}$ says /ī/ will give students the tool to correctly decode the word.

I was taught that $\boxed{\text{ch}}$ says /ch/. Until a few years ago, I had never realized

Table 1:   Single-Letter Phonograms

Phonogram	Sound	Sample Words			
a	/ă-ā-ä/	m*a*t	t*a*ble	f*a*ther	
b	/b/	*b*at			
c	/k-s/	*c*at	*c*ent		
d	/d/	*d*ad			
e	/ĕ-ē/	t*e*nt	b*e*		
f	/f/	*f*oot			
g	/g-j/	bi*g*	*g*ym		
h	/h/	*h*at			
i	/ĭ-ī-ē-y/	*i*t	*i*vy	stad*i*um	on*i*on
j	/j/	*j*ob			
k	/k/	*k*it			
l	/l/	*l*ap			
m	/m/	*m*e			
n	/n/	*n*ut			
o	/ŏ-ō-ö/	*o*n	g*o*	d*o*	
p	/p/	*p*an			
qu*	/kw/	*qu*een			
r	/r/	*r*an			
s	/s-z/	*s*ent	a*s*		
t	/t/	*t*ip			
u	/ŭ-ū-ö-ü/	*u*p	p*u*pil	fl*u*te**	p*u*t
v	/v/	*v*an			
w	/w/	*w*all			
x	/ks-z/	fo*x*	*x*ylophone		
y	/y-ĭ-ī-ē/	*y*ard	g*y*m	b*y*	bab*y*
z	/z/	*z*ip			

* Q is always written with a U. Technically it is a multi-letter phonogram.

** In many words long /ū/ drops the first /y/ sound and sounds like /ö/. (Compare *cute* and *flute*.)

that it actually says three sounds, /ch-k-sh/. The word *school* was always a complete mystery to me, not to mention *Christmas*. French words such as *chef, machine,* and *crochet* were at first difficult to read and later difficult to spell. Simply knowing all three sounds provided clarity where confusion had reigned.

Many educators mistakenly believe that good readers read whole words rather than reading phonetically. The prevailing thought is that readers who sound out words are slow, and that fast readers have actually developed instant recognition of the whole word. This is some of the theory behind the Dolch List, a commonly used list of 250 sight words.

However, recent research using functional MRI has shown that good readers are actually processing the sounds one at time, even though they perceive it as a whole word.[1] It is just that the brain is so fast, it appears they are reading whole words. In reality, though, they are converting the letters on the page to sounds.

These studies have shown that the brain learns to read the same way it learns to talk—one sound at a time. Once students get the hang of reading the sounds, they speed up until it appears to be instantaneous. As one researcher concluded, "The use of intensive phonics is the only way to teach dyslexics and learning disabled individuals how to read and is the best way for everyone to learn to read."[2]

This type of research further demonstrates the importance of teaching the 74 basic phonograms to all English speakers. The 74 basic phonograms are the most essential because they are the ones needed to spell the most frequently used words in English. They explain 98% of English words and are vital building blocks. The 74 basic phonograms should be taught thoroughly and systematically to all students from the beginning. They should not be reserved only for struggling students who make it to specialized reading centers.

Learning the 74 basic phonograms is the true foundation for literacy and spelling. Mastering the phonograms only occurs with regular practice over time. Just as students need to memorize math facts like 1+1=2, these phonograms need to be memorized as well. There are plenty of games and methods to contextualize this kind of drill and make it interesting, fun, and effective.

For more ideas on how to teach the phonograms, see *The Phonogram and Spelling Game Book.*

Phonogram Aids for Spelling

The phonograms are best memorized first by sound. Once the sounds are familiar, the additional spelling aids introduced in Table 3 are helpful to learn as well. Most of the aids for spelling are derived from the rules which are covered in later chapters. The phonograms in Table 3 are grouped to highlight their relationships with one another. Many of the phonograms form pairs. Understanding their relationships and how the pairs are defined by spelling rules greatly reduces the difficulty of memorizing them.

Advanced Phonograms

When learning a complex language such as English, it is vital to study the most essential components first. English has an extensive vocabulary. Although no English speaker masters every word, everyone uses the most frequently used words. The 100 most frequently used words make up 50% of all written material, while the 300 most frequently used words make up 65%. This is because the most frequent words are basic grammatical words like *the, is, has, have, was, could*, etc. These words appear in every level of writing, from a simple children's book to a doctoral thesis.

The 74 basic phonograms are derived from the high frequency words. There are an additional 46 advanced phonograms listed in Appendix E. A phonogram may be classified as advanced if it does not occur early in high frequency word lists and if it represents a very limited number of words.

Students who understand the 74 basic phonograms easily recognize advanced ones within words. Many of the advanced phonograms are related to the 74 basic phonograms. For example aigh says /ā/. This is advanced because the only word that uses this phonogram is *straight*. Students who know the phonogram ai , /ā/, easily decode aigh, because ai and aigh are clearly related.

Table 2: Multi-Letter Phonogram Sounds

Phonogram	Sound	Sample Words		
ai	/ā/	laid		
ar	/är/	car		
au	/ä/	author		
augh	/ä-ăf/	taught	laugh	
aw	/ä/	saw		
ay	/ā/	play		
bu	/b/	buy		
ch	/ch-k-sh/	child	school	chef
cei	/sē/	receive		
ci	/sh/	spacious		
ck	/k/	back		
dge	/j/	edge		
ea	/ē-ĕ-ā/	eat	bread	steak
ear	/er/	search		
ed	/ĕd-d-t/	traded	pulled	picked
ee	/ē/	tree		
ei	/ā-ē-ī/	their	protein	feisty
eigh	/ā-ī/	eight	height	
er	/er/	her		
ew	/ö-ū/	flew	few	
ey	/ā-ē/	they	key	
gn	/n/	sign		
gu	/g-gw/	guide	language	
ie	/ē/	field		

Phonogram	Sound	Sample Words		
igh	/ī/	ni*gh*t		
ir	/er/	b*ir*d		
kn	/n/	*kn*ow		
ng	/ng/	si*ng*		
oa	/ō/	c*oa*t		
oe	/ō-ö/	t*oe*	sh*oe*	
oi	/oi/	b*oi*l		
oo	/ö-ü-ō/	f*oo*d	t*oo*k	fl*oo*r
or	/ōr/	l*or*d		
ou	/ow-ō-ö-ŭ-ü/	h*ou*se *c*ou*ntry*	s*ou*l c*ou*ld	gr*ou*p
ough	/ŏ-ō-ö-ow-ŭf-ŏf/	th*ough*t b*ough*	th*ough* r*ough*	thr*ough* tr*ough*
ow	/ow-ō/	pl*ow*	sn*ow*	
oy	/oi/	b*oy*		
ph	/f/	*ph*one		
sh	/sh/	*sh*e		
si	/sh-zh/	ses*si*on	divi*si*on	
tch	/ch/	bu*tch*er		
th	/th-TH/	*th*in	*th*is	
ti	/sh/	par*ti*al		
ui	/ö/	fr*ui*t		
ur	/er/	h*ur*ts		
wh	/wh/	*wh*isper		
wor	/wer/	*wor*m		
wr	/r/	*wr*ite		

Table 3:   Multi-Letter Phonogram Spelling Aids

Phonogram	Sound	Aids
ai	/ā/	Two letter /ā/ that **may not** be used at the end of English words.
ay	/ā/	Two letter /ā/ that **may** be used at the end of English words.
au	/ä/	Two letter /ä/ that **may not** be used at the end of English words.
augh	/ä-ăf/	Used only at the end of a base word or before a T.
aw	/ä/	Two letter /ä/ that **may** be used at the end of English words.
ar	/är/	
bu	/b/	Two letter /b/.
cei	/sē/	
ch	/ch-k-sh/	
ck	/k/	Two letter /k/ used only after a single, short vowel.
dge	/j/	Hard /j/ used only after a single, short vowel.
ea	/ē-ĕ-ā/	
ear	/er/	The /er/ of search.
er	/er/	The /er/ of her.
ir	/er/	The /er/ of bird.
ur	/er/	The /er/ of hurt.
ed	/ĕd-d-t/	Past tense ending.
ee	/ē/	Double /ē/.
ei	/ā-ē-ī/	**May not** be used at the end of English words.
eigh	/ā-ī/	Used only at the end of a base word or before a T.
ey	/ā-ē/	**May** be used at the end of English words.
ew	/ö-ū/	**May** be used at the end of English words.
gn	/n/	Two letter /n/ used at the beginning or the end of a base word.
kn	/n/	Two letter /n/ used only at the beginning of a base word.
gu	/g-gw/	

Phonogram	Sound	Aids
ie	/ē/	The /ē/ of field.
igh	/ī/	Three letter /ī/ used only at the end of a base word or before a T.
ng	/ng/	
oa	/ō/	**May not** be used at the end of English words.
oe	/ō-ŏ/	**May** be used at the end of English words.
oi	/oi/	**May not** be used at the end of English words.
oy	/oi/	**May** be used at the end of English words.
oo	/ö-ü-ō/	
or	/ōr/	
ow	/ow-ō/	**May** be used at the end of English words.
ou	/ow-ō-ö-ŭ-ü/	**May not** be used at the end of English words.
ough	/ŏ-ō-ö-ow-ŭf-ŏf/	Used only at the end of a base word or before a T.
ph	/f/	Two letter /f/.
sh	/sh/	Used only at the beginning of a word and at the end of a syllable. Never used at the beginning of any syllable after the first one, except for the ending -ship.
si	/sh-zh/	Used only at the beginning of any syllable after the first one.
ci	/sh/	Short /sh/ used only at the beginning of any syllable after the first one.
ti	/sh/	Tall /sh/ used only at the beginning of any syllable after the first one.
tch	/ch/	Three letter /ch/ used after a single vowel that is not long.
th	/th-TH/	
ui	/ö/	Two letter /ö/ that **may not** be used at the end of English words.
wh	/wh/	Used only at the beginning of a base word.
wor	/wer/	
wr	/r/	Two letter /r/ used only at the beginning of a base word.

Chapter 4

CONSONANTS, VOWELS, AND SYLLABLES

What They Are and Why They Matter

Consonants and Vowels

Most English speakers have memorized the vowels: A, E, I, O, U, and sometimes Y. However, I have seldom met anyone who knows the definitions of *vowel* and *consonant*. It is also rare for people to know how this knowledge contributes to the formation of syllables. Fewer yet can explain how knowing these basics will help them spell and read. Nevertheless, understanding consonants, vowels, and syllables is essential to reading and spelling.

First, what is a vowel? A **vowel** is a sound that is produced when the mouth is open and the sound is not blocked by the lips, teeth, or tongue. Vowels are sounds that can be sustained, as in singing, and controlled for volume. To say a vowel sound, we must open our mouths. It is this opening that forms syllables.

Consonants on the other hand are sounds which are blocked by the tongue, teeth, or lips in some way. Most of them are difficult to sing or control for volume.

It is very simple to identify consonants and vowels. Simply try to sing or shout the sounds. If a sound can easily be sung or shouted **and** your mouth is open, it is a vowel. For example, /ă/. This sound can be sung and shouted, and the mouth is open. If it cannot be sung or shouted, such as /b/, it is a consonant. Be careful to isolate the /b/ sound; it is not pronounced /bŭ/, which would be spelled with the two phonograms, ⬚ b and ⬚ u . Some students want to classify /m/ as a vowel, because it can be sung. The mouth, however, is closed. The definition of a vowel is that the mouth is open and the sound can be sustained, as if it were being sung.

If you perform this simple test on all 74 phonograms, you will discover English has 15 vowel sounds. They are /ă, ā, ä, ĕ, ē, ĭ, ī, ŏ, ō, oo, ŭ, ū, ü, oi, ow/.*
Vowels are essential to language. To demonstrate this, try to yell for help without the vowel sound (/hlp/!). It is impossible.

Vowels create the most difficulty for reading and spelling in English. This is partially due to the fact that English is a vowel-rich language. Moreover, English has 28 ways to write the 15 vowel sounds, and most of the vowel phonograms can make more than one of the 15 sounds. To make matters even worse, the vowels are what vary the most among dialects and are typically not pronounced clearly the way they are spelled. For more information on vowels, see Chapter 16.

Syllables

English is a rhythmic language. The rhythm is formed by syllables. A **syllable** is an uninterrupted segment of sound which is formed by the opening and closing of the mouth to form vowels. When we count the number of syllables, we are also counting the number of vowel sounds. Knowing how many syllables are in a word and where the syllable breaks occur greatly aids spelling.

One of the easiest ways to learn to count syllables is to place your hand under your chin and count the number of times your mouth opens. If this fails, hum the word. For example: *table* would be hm-hm, whereas *museum* is hm-hm-hm.

---

* Technically the long vowels /ā, ē, ī, ō, and ū/ as well as /ö/, /oi/, and /ow/ are diphthongs. A diphthong is two vowel sounds that are heard in one syllable. Since the average student of English associates long /ā/ as one vowel sound, for simplicity *Uncovering the Logic of English* also classifies diphthongs as one vowel, though in reality they represent two sounds.

Because syllables are formed by vowels, every syllable has only one vowel sound you can hear. This does not mean that every syllable has only one single-letter vowel. Many of the vowels are multi-letter phonograms, which represent one vowel sound. For example, *taunt* has one vowel sound /ä/ written with the two letters A and U.

Finally, every syllable must have a written vowel. In most words, L and R behave as typical consonants. However, the sounds /l/ and /r/ are similar to vowels in that they can be sustained. Though the sound is blocked by the tongue, there is less obstruction than with the other consonants. This means that /l/ and /r/ sometimes form a new syllable without a vowel sound. This occurs at the end of a word. Consider words such as *ta-ble, waf-fle, a-cre*, etc. Since every syllable must have a written vowel, a silent final E is added. See Chapter 7.

Understanding the difference between a consonant and a vowel and knowing how to identify syllables is foundational to spelling. These concepts are built upon by the spelling rules and are essential to understanding the logic of English.

Chapter 5

FOUNDATIONAL CONSONANT RULES

M ost English speakers do not believe English has reliable spelling rules. Too often they were taught oversimplifications that only explained a small percentage of English words. For example, a commonly taught rule is "When two vowels go walking, the first one does the talking." Students are left wondering which sound of the first vowel should be used. Long /ē/ as in *heat* or short /ĕ/ as in *head*? This "rule" also does not account for words such as *great*, where the second vowel does the talking. These sorts of oversimplifications often generate more exceptions than words which follow the rule. Nevertheless, there are better rules which help to explain 98% of English words. These rules are carefully worded to provide clarity to the established patterns in English.

There are three types of spelling rules:

1) Rules that limit the usage of one or more given phonogram(s),
2) Rules that control how suffixes are added to words, and
3) Rules that explain which sound of a phonogram is heard based upon other patterns within the word.

Letters may represent a sound, change the sound of another phonogram, or both at the same time. A **diacritic** is a phonogram that affects the sound of another phonogram by its proximity. For example, the silent final E in *ripe* informs the reader to read long /ī/ rather than short /ĭ/ as in *rip*. It is much more efficient to summarize diacritics as rules rather than to categorize each possibility as a new phonogram.

English is not the only language in which the proximity of phonograms causes them to affect one another. In fact, some English rules, such as "C always softens to /s/ when followed by an E, I, or Y" (Rule 1), are found in most of the Latin-based languages. Knowing that these sorts of patterns are present in English teaches students to recognize them in other languages as well.

The study of Latin has long been used as a tool to aid students' understanding of how languages are structured at a sentence level. Likewise, the English language is an excellent vehicle for learning the word structure of languages. Think of English as a complex language puzzle. Once students discover the patterns and realize they are consistent, they will have the tools not only to read and spell in English, but to tackle other languages as well.

This chapter covers the three foundational consonant rules. These simple rules clearly explain some of the most commonly misspelled words and resolve what are usually thought of as impossible exceptions. These rules continue to reappear in subsequent chapters as the reasons underlying other rules.

Rule 1

Do you know why *picnic* is spelled with a C at the end, but a K is added to *picnicking*? Or how about *mimic* and *mimicking*?

I have asked the same questions to hundreds of teachers in the past few years. In my experience, less than 1% have answered it correctly, and fewer than 5% even knew we needed to add a K. We can clearly see how deeply broken our education system has become when the answer to this question is a rule which explains more than 9,000 words.*

Strong spellers typically rely on a word "looking right" to know if it is spelled correctly. These people are visual learners and frequently need to write down the word so they can see it. *Picnicking* and *mimicking* are examples where even strong visual learners struggle when they do not understand the rules of English.

---

* www.morewords.com: 4,000 examples for *ce*, more than 4,000 for *ci*, and 1,124 containing *cy*.

This first rule should be common knowledge to English speakers:

Rule 1   C always softens to /s/ when followed by E, I, or Y.
Otherwise, C says /k/.

Without the added K, *picnicing* would be pronounced /pĭc nĭ sĭng/, because the C says /s/ before an I. The K is inserted to protect the hard /k/ sound. The same is true of *mimicking*. Before we expand on what is occurring in *picnicking* and *mimicking*, we will explore the rule in more depth.

First, C always softens to /s/ before E, I, and Y:

center	circus	icy
accent	accident	agency
nitroglycerin	ancillary	cynicism

Next, let's consider when C says its hard sound. C says /k/:

- before the other vowels: A, O, U:

cat	cot	cut
California	balcony	speculate
abdicate	abscond	culinary

- before a consonant:

clap	cranberry	enacting

- at the end of the word:

arc	pathetic	acoustic

This rule explains simple words and complex words. Once you know it, you will begin to see it everywhere. It greatly clarifies how to read words that contain a C, for it clearly explains when C will say /k/ and when it will say /s/.

It also clearly explains why, in words such as *circus, cycle,* and *accent,* C can say both /k/ and /s/.

This knowledge is also useful for spelling. Last week a seven-year-old I tutor used this rule to correct her own spelling. She was writing the word *make.* She initially wrote *mace.* She paused, then unprompted, erased the C and replaced it with a K. She saw that the C said /s/ before the E and knew that she needed to use K instead. The same process this young student used can be applied to words at all levels of English vocabulary.

Let's return to the word *picnicking.* Knowing C says /s/ only before E, I, and Y also aids us when adding the common endings *-ing, -ed,* and *-y* to words which end with C. We must add K to protect the C from softening to /s/.

Root	Root plus ending	Root	Root plus ending
picnic	picnicking	frolic	frolicking
mimic	mimicking	politic	politicking
colic	colicky	traffic	trafficked
garlic	garlicky	panic	panicked

Now when your spell-checker underlines one of these commonly mis-spelled words, you have the tool to fix it. Remember though to add a K only if the hard sound /k/ is heard in the derivative. Some words soften the C to /s/ with the ending.

Root	Root plus ending	Root	Root plus ending
critic	criticism	toxic	toxicity

Interestingly, native English words prevent the need for adding K before the common endings *-ing, -ed,* and *-y* by having a spelling of /k/ which insulates the C: ck .

Root	Root plus ending	Root	Root plus ending
pack	packing	peck	pecking
trick	tricky	luck	lucky

True Exceptions

These rules describe 98% of English words. This means there are a few exceptions. However, they are truly exceptional. When a word breaks a common pattern it is now notable and worthy of comment. Interestingly, many of the exceptions to this rule are also explainable.

Arcing, soccer—In these two words, the C is before an I or E and would normally soften to /s/. However, the hard /k/ sound is retained.

Celtics—Although we commonly pronounce this word /kĕl-tĭks/ when referring to something from the Celtic culture, our pronunciation conforms to the spelling rule when we refer to the sports team the Boston Celtics.

Caesar—This word is derived from Latin and is spelled using the advanced phonogram ⬚ae⬚ which says /ē/. Though the C is before a written A, it is followed by the sound /ē/ and likewise softens to /s/.

Cello, ciao—These are both Italian words. Italian words also soften the C before an E and I; however, the soft form in Italian is /ch/. This pronunciation was retained.

Connecticut, indict—Both contain a silent C.

Facade—In French these words are spelled with a cédille for /s/. English retained the foreign spelling and pronunciation; however, ç is not a character in our alphabet.

Rule 2

This next rule is obviously related to the previous one. However, there is one key difference.

Rule 2	G may soften to /j/ only when followed by E, I, or Y. Otherwise, G says /g/.

germ	ginger	biology
angelic	agile	allergy

The difference is: G **may** say /j/ . . . It does **not always**. It is important to phrase rules carefully so they account for the actual lexicon of English and do not create false expectations.

G is the only single-letter phonogram which spells the sound /g/. Therefore in a few words, G retains its hard sound /g/ before E, I, or Y.

get	gift	gynecology
anger	begin	argyle

Do not hastily discard this rule because it is not an absolute. This rule states: the only time G does say /j/ is when it is followed by an E, I, or Y. When G is not followed by an E, I, or Y, it must say /g/:

- before the vowels A, O, U,

gap	goat	begun
cardigan	archipelago	configure

- before a consonant,

glad	granular	magnet

- and at the end of the word

egg	crag	leg

Italian words insert a silent letter $\boxed{h}$ to separate the G from an E or an I to retain the hard /g/ sound, forming the advanced phonogram $\boxed{gh}$.

ghetto	spaghetti

French and Spanish words insert a silent letter $\boxed{\text{u}}$ to separate the G from E or I to retain the hard /g/ sound, forming the phonogram $\boxed{\text{gu}}$.

| plague | guide | guerilla | guitar |

This rule also helps to explain the multi-letter phonogram $\boxed{\text{dge}}$. G is followed by an E, causing the G to say /j/.[*]

Rule 3

This next rule is foundational to the silent final E rules. I will introduce the consonant portion briefly here and revisit the vowel portion in Chapter 6.

| **Rule 3** | English words do not end in I, U, V, or J. |

The fact that English words do not end in V is essential to understanding the second most common reason for a silent final E. For more information, see Chapter 7.

English words also do not end in J. When the sound /j/ is heard at the end of the word, there are two common spellings. The first is the multi-letter phonogram $\boxed{\text{dge}}$ as in:

| edge | smudge | dodge | knowledge |

The second is G followed by a silent final E. For more information, see Chapter 7.

| large | age | change | marriage |

---

[*] For astute speakers of English, the sound represented by the phonogram DGE in words such as **edge, fudge, hedge** is slightly stronger than the sound represented by the pure /j/ sound as in **jam, junk, garage, marriage**. For simplicity, these sounds will be considered the same in *Uncovering the Logic of English*.

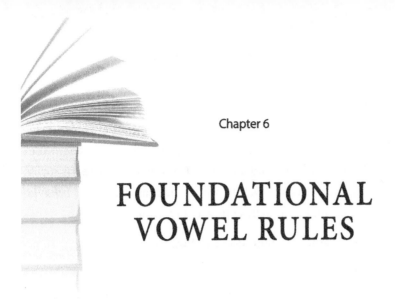

Chapter 6

FOUNDATIONAL
VOWEL RULES

E nglish is a challenging language to spell and read, primarily due to the vowels. There are three difficulties with vowels. First, we have been misled to believe English has only 10 vowel sounds: short and long sounds for A, E, I, O, and U. In reality, English has 15 vowel sounds and 28 written phonograms which represent these sounds. Second, 16 of the vowel phonograms say more than one sound. Third, it is the vowel sounds that are most distorted in speech, vary the most between dialects, and often shift in pronunciation with the addition of prefixes and suffixes.

Thankfully, there are rules which govern some of the vowels. These rules are foundational and help to explain a majority of English words. Vowel rules play two primary roles: first, they determine which vowel sound will be heard within a given word. Second, they limit the usage of particular vowel spellings.

Before we continue, let's review the definition of a vowel. A vowel is a sound that is produced with an open mouth. Vowels can be sustained, as in singing, and controlled for volume.

Each of the single-letter vowels A, E, I, O, and U represents a long and short vowel sound. A, O, and U also make a third sound which is called the broad sound (see Table 4). Together the single vowels represent 13 vowel sounds.

English also has a mysterious single letter vowel commonly learned as "sometimes Y." Y is both a consonant and a vowel. It has four sounds /y-ĭ-ī-ē/

which we can categorize as consonants or vowels through the singing test. Because /y/ cannot be sung, it is a consonant sound. Since we are able to sing /ĭ/, /ī/, and /ē/, these are vowel sounds. In addition, though it is not commonly known, I also acts as both a vowel and a consonant. In words where I is saying the sound /ĭ/, /ī/, and /ē/, it is a vowel. In words such as *onion* and *behavior* where it says the /y/ sound, I is actually acting as a consonant.

Table 4:   Single-Letter Vowels

Phonogram	Sound	Examples			
a	/ă-ā-ä/	m*a*t	t*a*ble	f*a*ther	
e	/ĕ-ē/	t*e*nt	b*e*		
i	/ĭ-ī-ē/	*i*t	*i*vy	stad*i*um	
o	/ŏ-ō-ö/	*o*n	g*o*	d*o*	
u	/ŭ-ū-ö-ü/	*u*p	p*u*pil	fl*u*te*	p*u*t
y	/ĭ-ī-ē/	g*y*m	b*y*	bab*y*	

English also has 22 multi-letter vowel phonograms. These are isolated in Table 5. Twelve of these make only one sound, five make two sounds, and the other five make three or more sounds.

Table 5:   Multi-Letter Vowels

Phonogram	Sound	Examples
ai	/ā/	l*ai*d
au	/ä/	*au*thor
aw	/ä/	s*aw*
ay	/ā/	pl*ay*
ee	/ē/	tr*ee*
ie	/ē/	p*ie*ce

---

* In many words, long /ū/ drops the /y/ sound and is pronounced simply /ö/.

igh	/ī/	ni*gh*t				
oa	/ō/	c*oa*t				
oi	/oi/	b*oi*l				
oy	/oi/	b*oy*				
ui	/ö/	fr*ui*t				
augh*	/ä/	t*augh*t				
eigh	/ā-ī/	*eigh*t	h*eigh*t			
ew	/ö-ū/	fl*ew*	f*ew*			
ey	/ā-ē/	th*ey*	k*ey*			
oe	/ō-ö/	t*oe*	sh*oe*			
ow	/ow-ō/	pl*ow*	sn*ow*			
ea	/ē-ĕ-ā/	*ea*t	br*ea*d	st*ea*k		
ei	/ā-ē-ī/	r*ei*n	prot*ei*n	f*ei*sty		
oo	/ö-ü-ō/	f*oo*d	t*oo*k	fl*oo*r		
ou	/ow-ō-ö-ŭ-ü/	h*ou*se	s*ou*l	gr*ou*p	c*ou*ntry	c*ou*ld
ough*	/ŏ-ō-ö-ow/	th*ough*t	th*ough*	thr*ough*	b*ough*	

English words do not end in I

We will now turn to the vowel portion of Rule 3. This is a powerful rule which is used repeatedly throughout English spelling.

Rule 3	English words do not end in I, U, V, or J.

At first glance, this rule may not appear particularly significant. Yet it is a thread woven throughout the phonograms, the silent final E rules, and rules for adding suffixes. Knowing this simple rule brings clarity to spelling and decoding.

---

* AUGH has two commonly heard sounds and OUGH has six commonly heard sounds. Only the pure vowel sounds are included on this chart.

First we will consider the ramifications of the fact that English words do not end in I, and then we will explore the impact of words not ending in U.

At the end of the chapter, we will consider some exceptions and how the rule provides insight into these words.

The rule that English words do not end in I governs one of the most intricate relationships in English: the relationship between I and Y.

The I/Y relationship is first seen in their shared **vowel** sounds.

	i	*y*
/ĭ/	mitt	myth
	Jim	gym
/ī/	kind	rhyme
	line	type
/ē/	piano	lady
	radius	ability

I and Y also share the **consonant** sound: /y/.

	i	*y*
/y/	union	yarn
	onion	yesterday
	opinion	lawyer
	brilliant	canyon

Based solely upon their sounds, /ĭ-ī-ē/ and /y/, I and Y are clearly related phonograms.

Because English words do not end in I, Y covers for I at the end of English words. Whenever the vowel sound /ī/ is heard at the end of the word, Y must be written instead.

cry   try   my

Three phonogram pairs end in I and Y: ⟨ay⟩ and ⟨ai⟩, ⟨ey⟩ and ⟨ei⟩, and ⟨oy⟩ and ⟨oi⟩. The rule that "English words do not end in I" governs these phonogram pairs. The phonograms which end in Y **may** be used at the end of English words. The phonograms that end in I **may not** be used at the end of English words. Once again, this is because English words do not end in I.

	May use at the end of English words	May **not** use at the end of English words
ay/ai	tray	disdain
ey/ei	they	vein
oy/oi	toy	toil

Only the **may not** forms of these phonogram pairs are restricted from being used at the end of words. The **may** forms have no restrictions and are found at the beginning, middle and end of words.

oyster	m**ay**or	surv**ey**

The relationship between I and Y will continue to unfold in Chapter 9 as we consider how the Y changes back to an I in words like *babies* and *babied*.

English words do not end in U

Let's now turn to the remaining vowel phonogram limited by rule 3: U.

Three multi-letter phonogram pairs end in U and W: ⟨aw⟩ and ⟨au⟩, ⟨ow⟩ and ⟨ou⟩, and ⟨ew⟩ and ⟨eu⟩.* Phonograms ending in U **may not** be used at the end of English words. The alternative spelling is the phonogram ending with W, which **may** be used at the end of words.

---

* EU is an advanced phonogram because it does not occur in the most commonly used words.

	May use at the end of English words	May **not** use at the end of English words
aw/au	saw	saucer
ow/ou	cow	count
ew/eu	flew	neutral

Once again, only the **may not** form is limited because English words do not end in U. The **may** form is also found at the beginning and in the middle of words.

own   bowl   awning   shawl

The fact that English words do not end in U is one of the most common reasons for adding a silent final E to English words. See Chapter 7.

True Exceptions

Foreign Words

Maybe you have already thought of a list of words ending in I and U. There are quite a few. Before you throw the rule out as another example of inconsistent phonics, however, it is important to listen to the rule closely. **English** words do not end in I or U. This is vitally important because most of the words which are "exceptions" are actually foreign words which have been brought into the language.

Even young students become very adept at noticing these words. One six-year-old girl cried out to her mom as they were driving, "Look, Mom, Jujitsu! That's not an English word!" She was right.

Knowing this rule greatly aids spelling of native English words and heightens our awareness that English is a multicultural language. Knowing that **English** words do not end in I or U cues us to ask, "What is the origin of the word?" In addition it helps us realize the word may not behave like native English words when adding suffixes.

Here are a few examples of words that are exceptions and their origins. This list is not intended to be exhaustive. Most of the words refer directly to other cultures and therefore retain foreign spellings.

Table 6:   Foreign Words Ending in I

Foreign Words Ending in I	Origin
chai	Arabic and Russian
macaroni, pastrami, broccoli	Italian
alibi, fungi	Latin
Helsinki	Finnish
calamari	Greek
bonsai, sushi, origami	Japanese
kiwi	Maori (New Zealand)
ski	Norwegian
Mississippi	Ojibwe and Algonquian

Table 7:   Foreign Words Ending in U

Foreign Words Ending in U	Origin
caribou	Algonquian
milieu, menu, impromptu	French
Honolulu	Hawaiian
tiramisu	Italian
tofu	Japanese
guru	Sanskrit

Table 8:   Slang Words Ending in I and U

Word	Abbreviation or Slang
hello	hi
taxicab	taxi
influenza	flu
through	thru

I, You, and Thou

Finally, the most common exceptions are the three very old English words: *I, you* and *thou*. I help students remember these exceptions by telling them: "You and I are very special."

Vowels at the End of Syllables

Now we will turn to another important rule which governs English vowels: the most common reason for a vowel to say its long sound. Unfortunately, most English speakers can identify only one reason for a single vowel to say its long sound: before a silent final E. Nevertheless, silent E's are not the most common reason. When incomplete phonics is taught, students are left believing they have all the possible tools, only to find that the tools do not work.

This next rule explains the most common reason for a single vowel to say its long sound. It applies to hundreds of thousands of words.

Rule 4   A E O U usually say their names at the end of a syllable.

fa mous	de sire	o pen	u nit
ba sin	be fore	ro bot	hu man

Conversely, this means vowels usually say their first or short sound when they are found in the middle of the syllable. Syllables always divide between double consonants. Since the vowel is no longer at the end of the syllable, the vowel says its short sound. Knowing this rule helps to clarify many commonly mispronounced and misspelled words.

ta per	tap per
be low	bel low
to paz	top ple
cu bic	cub by

Did you notice that the last rule covered all the single letter vowels except I and Y? These two follow slightly different rules:

Rule 5   I and Y may say /ĭ/ or /ī/ at the end of a syllable.

	I	*Y*
ĭ	cli nic	phy sic al
	pro hi bi tion	cy nic
ī	li on	cry
	vi o lin	ty po

Sometimes double consonants are added to distinguish these words as well. Notice that the syllable is always divided between the double consonants so that the short sound /ĭ/ is heard in the middle.

di ner	din ner

> **Rule 6**   When a one-syllable word ends in a single vowel Y,
>   it says /ī/.

This rule only applies to one syllable words ending in a single vowel Y. It does not apply to the multi-letter phonograms ay , ey , and oy .

by	my	try
why	fry	fly

This rule also does not limit the pronunciation of Y in multisyllable words. Y does say /ī/ at the end of a few multisyllable words and with the suffix -ify.

apply	simplify
deny	horrify

> **Rule 7**   Y says /ē/ only at the end of a multi-syllable word.

baby	happy	berry
charity	ability	archeology

This rule is only limiting where Y says the long /ē/ sound. Y may also say /ī/ at the end of a multisyllable word, though the long /ē/ sound is heard in a vast majority of multisyllable words ending in Y.

Many people are surprised to discover that the letter I may also say the long /ē/ sound. This commonly occurs in two places. First, at the end of a syllable that is followed by a vowel such as:

sta di um	ra di us	o lym pi an
ra di ator	he li um	pi an o

Second, I may say the long /ē/ sound at the end of foreign words, such as:

spaghetti   pastrami   Helsinki

The rule which governs I saying long /ē/ is summarized in the second part of Rule 7:

Rule 7 I says /ē/ at the end of a syllable that is followed by a vowel and at the end of foreign words.

Spellings for Long I and Long O

Rule 8 I and O may say /ī/ and /ō/ when followed by two consonants.

Long /ō/	Short /ŏ/	Long /ī/	Short /ĭ/
bold	bond	pint	print
poll	pond	rind	rink

This rule is carefully worded to not set false expectations. *I and O **may say** /ī/ and /ō/.* . . Students need to be alerted to the reason for I and O saying their long sounds within these words yet understand that it does not happen in every word. When students know this rule, they have the necessary knowledge to understand their options when reading words that follow this form.

Spellings for /ā/ and /ä/

Phonics programs often only teach the short and long sounds for the phonogram a . The problem is that this leaves very simple words like *ma* and *pa* to be memorized as sight words. Knowing all the phonograms and the following rules aids decoding many words and limits the options for spelling.

Rule 9	AY usually spells the sound /ā/ at the end of a base word.

AY Spells /ā/

may

por tray

pay

dis may

There are only ten commonly known words which use the phonogram ey to spell the long sound /ā/ at the end of the word. These are: *they, convey, obey, hey, ley, osprey, prey, purvey, survey* and *whey.*[*] Each is accounted for by the careful wording in Rule 9: AY **usually** spells /ā/. Students should learn the ten EY words as a group. Once they memorize this list, all other words that say /ā/ at the end of the word are spelled AY.

Rule 10	When a word ends with the phonogram A, it says /ä/. A may also say /ä/ after a W or before an L.

A Says Its Third Sound /ä/

ma

ze bra

ven det ta

stam i na

---

[*] The British spelling for *grey* also uses the phonogram EY (Appendix J).

It is amazing how consistent these rules are. Rule 10 applies to 2,929 words ending with A that say /ä/, and Rule 9 applies to 298 words ending with AY that say /ā/.[1]

The Phonogram QU

Rule 11   Q always needs a U; therefore, U is not a vowel here.

The multi-letter phonogram ⟨ qu ⟩ says /kw/. It is always written with two letters. This is important to understand because U does not form a vowel sound or count as a written vowel for the syllable. This will be necessary to understand when adding suffixes. (See page 81.)

queen   **qu**it   **qu**ality

Exceptions

Foreign spellings usually follow this rule, though there are a few exceptions imported from Arabic. For example: *Iraq*.

Knowing the consonant and vowel rules greatly reduces frustration in reading and spelling. Since determining which vowel sound is heard in particular words is one of the most frustrating problems for young readers, learning these basic rules will provide immediate help for decoding. The rules are equally as powerful for spelling. Although English is a complex language at the word level, knowing these simple rules illuminates the pronunciation of these words and demonstrates there is a method behind what at first appears to be sheer madness.

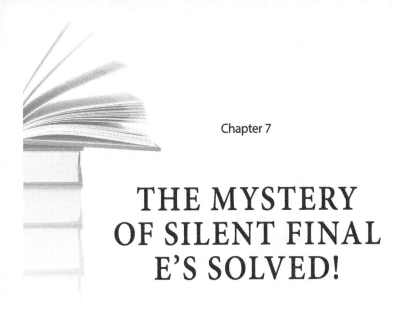

Chapter 7

THE MYSTERY OF SILENT FINAL E'S SOLVED!

Silent final E's are one of the most frustrating aspects of English. They seem to appear out of nowhere. Everyone knows that they are used to make the vowel sound long, but there are at least as many silent final E's that do not affect the vowel.

For new readers this is terribly confusing. We teach the rule "The vowel says its name because of the E," and the first real book the child reads is riddled with apparent exceptions: *have, dance, give, love, move, loose,* and on and on. We seem to be constantly telling new readers, "That is an exception."

When I taught my intuitive daughter to read, she seemed to blow past all these "exceptions" without concern. She used the inconsistent rules as an approximation and proceeded to memorize each individual word. Since she does not have a photographic memory, this caused her a great deal of trouble with spelling.

On the other hand, my logically and literally minded students consistently applied the only silent final E rule I taught them—"The vowel says its name because of the E"—until they proved to themselves and to me that I was wrong. Then they lost interest in reading.

In addition to causing headaches for decoding, silent E's represent two of the most common spelling mistakes. Many students think E's are randomly tacked to the end of words, so they add extras ad hoc. Other students forget to add E's where they are needed.

What is the solution? Fortunately, knowing the reasons for adding silent final E's simplifies both decoding and spelling. These rules are powerful tools which most students, educators, and even linguists do not know. Yet knowing the purpose for silent final E's revolutionizes spelling and reading!

In the following pages I will introduce nine types of silent final E's. They are listed in the order of frequency. The first four types explain a majority of silent final E's and are the most important for young students. To highlight what is occurring within each word, the reason for the E is in bold, the silent final E is underlined twice, and a small number corresponding to the type of E is written next to the word.

Type 1: Long Vowels

The most common and well known reason for a silent E is to change the vowel sound from short to long. This type occurs in 50% of words with a silent final E.

> **Rule 12.1** The vowel says its long sound because of the E.

cape₁   pipe₁   type₁   bone₁   cute₁*

This also may occur with two consonants separating the vowel from the silent E.

paste₁   clothe₁   change₁   waste₁   strange₁

---

* In words like *tune*, the long /ū/ often loses the /y/ sound that is part of its name when blended into words. Many students do not even notice that this is occurring because clearly enunciating /t-y-oo-n/ is so difficult. Therefore we exaggerate the sounds for spelling purposes and acknowledge that /y/ disappears when blended for speech.

Type 2: V and U

Before learning these rules, my engineering-minded students applied the rule *The vowel says its long sound . . .* to every silent E they encountered. This caused them to consistently misread words such as *give*: /gĭv/. Though I corrected them, each time they encountered a non–Type 1 silent E word, they misread it.

I became concerned when they were not able to recognize words after seeing them hundreds of times. I had been taught that phonics is a crutch that supports the brain as it moves to reading sight words. However, these students did not master reading when I tried to force them to memorize each word. Rather, they became increasingly frustrated with themselves, with me, and with English as they tried to apply inconsistent rules. However, once they were provided with phonograms and rules which worked, it was only a matter of time (for some only a few weeks) before they were able to decode fluently. It appeared as if they were reading sight words, but now they had the tools to sound out the words efficiently.

I experienced exactly what the latest brain research has told us about how the brain reads. The best readers decode every word, almost instantly.[1,2] The brain is simply not able to memorize thousands of "sight words."[3]

Learning all the reasons for silent final E's is one of the simplest and most helpful boosts for students struggling with reading and spelling.

Look at the following words. Do you see a pattern?

have₂	live₂	valve₂
mauve₂	additive₂	adjective₂
true₂	blue₂	argue₂
value₂	rescue₂	venue₂

Which consonant spelling rule dictates the need for a silent final E within these words? These words are not exceptions. The need for the E is related to the consonant spelling rule: English words do not end in I, U, V, or J. This is summarized by the Type 2 reason for a silent final E:

Rule 12.2 English words do not end in V or U.

Notice that without the E, words such as *hav* and *giv* can be sounded out just fine. The E is not present to change the pronunciation but to prevent the words from ending in V.

Without the E, words such as *tru* and *blu* also sound just fine. Since A, E, O, U usually say their name at the end of the syllable, each will end in the long /ū/ sound. The E is not needed to clue pronunciation; rather, it prevents the words from ending in U.

Knowing that English words do not end in V or U greatly reduces the amount of rote memory work for spelling. From now on, whenever you hear /v/ or /ū/ at the end of the word, add a silent E. This rule also provides answers about how to decode words that end in V silent E and U silent E.

Type 3: C and G

Type 3 is based on the consonant spelling rules: C says /s/ and G may say /j/ **only** before an E, I, or Y.

Look at each of the following examples. Pronounce each word with the E and then without the E. With the E the C says /s/. Without the E, C says /k/. This is because C says /s/ before E, I, or Y.

choice₃	force₃	voice₃
commerce₃	absence₃	abundance₃

Pronounce each word with the E and then without the E. With the E the G will say /j/. Without the E, G will say /g/. This is because G may say /j/ before E, I, or Y.

change₃	cage₃	barge₃
orange₃	avenge₃	language₃

In each of the words above, an E was added to soften the C and G. This is summarized by the rule:

Rule 12.3 The C says /s/ and the G says /j/ because of the E.

Type 4: Syllables

The sounds /l/ and /r/ are very similar to vowels. They can be sustained, yet the sound is partially blocked by the tongue. While the tongue does obstruct the sound, there is less obstruction than other consonants. Occasionally this results in /l/ and /r/ forming a new syllable without a heard vowel sound. When this occurs a silent E is added because:

Rule 12.4 Every syllable must have a written vowel.

The fourth type of silent final E applies to words ending in *-ble, -cle, -dle, -fle, -gle, -kle, -ple, -sle, -tle, -zle, -cre,* and *-tre.*

ta **ble**₄	bi cy **cle**₄	bun **dle**₄	waf **fle**₄
goo **gle**₄	frec **kle**₄	ma **ple**₄	has **sle**₄
tur **tle**₄	puz **zle**₄	a **cre**₄	cen **tre**₄

Comparing American and British Spellings

Type 4 silent final E's distinguish British and American spellings for several words. The standard American spelling uses the phonogram er , whereas the standard British spelling uses the phonogram r followed by a silent final E. The British spelling adds a silent final E because every syllable must have a written vowel.

American Spelling	British Spelling
cen ter	cen tre$_4$
lus ter	lus tre$_4$
spec ter	spec tre$_4$
fib er	fib re$_4$

Type 5: Distinguish Singular from Plural

Do you know why there is a silent E in words such as *house* and *goose?*

To understand the reason, pause and consider how English forms the plural form.

Singular Nouns	Plural Nouns
chair	chairs
table	tables
book	books

To form the plural, the suffix -*s* is added to the end of the base word. *Moose, house,* and *goose* are all singular words which end in the letter S. To keep singular words that end with /s/ from looking plural, a silent final E is added. This is summarized by:

> **Rule 12.5** Add an E to keep singular words that end in the letter S from looking plural.

house$_5$	mouse$_5$	purse$_5$
goose$_5$	moose$_5$	purchase$_5$

The same concept occurs with verbs. In English, an -S is added to denote the singular verb form. The plural verb is the root form of the verb.

Root	Singular Verbs	Plural Verbs
sit	He sits.	They sit.
play	She plays.	They play.
roll	Max rolls.	We roll.

When the root verb ends with an S, a silent final E is added to distinguish it from the singular verb form.

Root	Singular Verbs	Plural Verbs
tease₅	He teases.	They tease₅
please₅	She pleases.	We please₅
amuse₅	Max amuses.	We amuse₅

Type 6: To Make the Word Look Bigger

This next reason is a favorite among children:

> **Rule 12.6** Add an E to make the word look bigger.

Many two and three letter words have a silent final E to make them bigger.

awe₆   ewe₆   rye₆

owe₆   tie₆   are₆

Type 7: Voiced and Unvoiced TH

Compare the following words. Why is the silent final E needed?

breath	breathe₇
teeth	teethe₇
cloth	clothe₇
bath	bathe₇
loath	loathe₇

> **Rule 12.7** TH says its voiced sound /TH/ because of the E.

Here are a few more examples:

writhe₇	lathe₇
seethe₇	soothe₇
wreathe₇	scathe₇

Type 8: Clarify Meaning

> **Rule 12.8** Add an E to clarify meaning.

Silent final E's are sometimes added to distinguish homophones or to clarify pronunciation and meaning.

or	ore₈
teas	tease₈
hears	hearse₈

Type 9: Unseen Reason

Rule 12.9 Unseen reason.

In a few words there is no visible explanation for the silent E. The silent E holds a story that has been lost over time. Perhaps it is a remnant of an older pronunciation that is no longer in use, or a tradition that began in some other way. Whatever the original reason, however, there are only a few words that fall into this category.

done$_9$ come$_9$ some$_9$
giraffe$_9$ where$_9$ were$_9$

Adding Suffixes to Silent Final E Words

Now the fun begins. The next rule helps even the best visual spellers by demystifying some of the most commonly misspelled words such as *courageous* and *chargeable*.

When you know the reason for the silent final E within a given word, you will be able to use this knowledge to decide if the E needs to be kept or dropped when adding a suffix, thereby eliminating some of the most problematic exceptions to the language.

In my elementary days, I learned the rule: "Drop the E and add -ing." This helped me to correctly spell *living*, but it didn't help me spell *forcible* correctly. Some people learned a better version: "Drop the E when adding a vowel suffix." This rule explains words such as *styling* but leaves *chargeable* as an exception.

Here is a concise rule which provides the best explanation:

Rule 13 Drop the silent final E when adding a vowel suffix only if it is allowed by other spelling rules.

This rule leads us to two questions that must be asked when adding a suffix to silent final E words:

> Are we adding a vowel suffix?
> Is dropping the E allowed by other spelling rules?
>   C says /s/ before E, I, and Y.
>   G may say /j/ before E, I, and Y.

The E may be dropped only if the answer to both questions is "yes." If the answer is "no" to either question, the E must be retained.

Are we adding a vowel suffix?

First, silent final E words only lose the need for the E when adding a vowel suffix. A **vowel suffix** is an ending that begins with a vowel. For example: *-able, -ing, -ed, -ish,* and *-y.* In contrast, a **consonant suffix** begins with a consonant. For example: *-ly, -ness, -ful, -hood,* and *-ment.* In the following examples, notice why the E is needed and that it is always retained when adding a consonant suffix.

$$\text{like}_1 + \text{ly} \rightarrow \text{likely}$$
$$\text{achieve}_2 + \text{ment} \rightarrow \text{achievement}$$
$$\text{force}_3 + \text{ful} \rightarrow \text{forceful}$$
$$\text{puz zle}_4 + \text{ment} \rightarrow \text{puzzlement}$$
$$\text{amuse}_5 + \text{ment} \rightarrow \text{amusement}$$
$$\text{awe}_6 + \text{some} \rightarrow \text{awesome}$$

Is dropping the E allowed by other spelling rules?

Second, we must know if the E is needed to make the word conform to other spelling rules. The rules we need to be concerned about are:

1. C says /s/ before E, I, and Y.
2. G may say /j/ before E, I, and Y.

Consider each of the following examples, and ask the questions for each word.

like$_1$ + ing → liking   hope$_1$ + ing → hoping

have$_2$ + ing → having   achieve$_2$ + ed → achieved

puz zle$_4$ + ing → puz zling   tease$_5$ + ing → teasing

owe$_6$ + ing → owing   teethe$_5$ + ing → teething

In each of these words, both of the key questions may be answered with "yes." The added suffix begins with a vowel, and the E is not needed for a C or G. So the E may be dropped.

Carefully consider the following examples.

$$\text{notice}_3 + \text{ing} \rightarrow \text{noticing}$$

$$\text{service}_3 + \text{ed} \rightarrow \text{serviced}$$

Are we adding a vowel suffix? "Yes." Is dropping the E allowed by other spelling rules? "Yes." In this group of words the E may be dropped because the C will still say /s/ before the I and E.

When a word has a silent final E to make a C say /s/, it is vital when adding a vowel suffix to determine if the E needs to be retained to keep the C soft. Remember, C says /s/ **only** before E, I, or Y. This interplay of rules explains many commonly misspelled words.

Carefully consider the following examples using the questions for adding a suffix to silent final E words.

$$\text{notice}_3 + \text{able} \rightarrow \text{noticeable}$$

$$\text{service}_3 + \text{able} \rightarrow \text{serviceable}$$

Are we adding a vowel suffix? "Yes." Is dropping the E allowed by other spelling rules? "No, without the E the C would say /k/." Therefore, the E is retained.

This same principle applies to words that have a silent final E to soften the G. Remember, G may say /j/ **only** before E, I, or Y. Consider the following examples:

$$encourage_{\underline{3}} + \ ing \rightarrow encouraging$$
$$charge_{\underline{3}} + \ ing \rightarrow charging$$
$$advantage_{\underline{3}} + \ ed \rightarrow advantaged$$

Are we adding a vowel suffix? "Yes." Is dropping the E allowed by other spelling rules? "Yes, the G will still says its soft sound." Then drop the E and add the suffix.

Now, consider the following words using the questions for adding a suffix to silent final E words.

$$charge_{\underline{3}} + \ able \rightarrow chargeable$$

$$advantage_{\underline{3}} + \ ous \rightarrow advantageous$$

$$courage_{\underline{3}} + \ ous \rightarrow courageous$$

Are we adding a vowel suffix? "Yes." Is dropping the E allowed by other spelling rules? "No. Without the E the G would say /g/." Then do not drop the E.

True Exceptions

Although these rules are extremely consistent and help to explain tens of thousands of words, there are a few exceptions. They are, though, truly exceptional! These are the only known exceptions.

Type 1

Ninth and **wholly**—In *nine* and *whole* the E is needed to make the vowel say its name. In these words, the E is dropped even though we are adding a consonant suffix. It is retained according to the rule when adding the consonant suffixes *-ty* and *-some* in the derivatives *ninety* and *wholesome*.

Mileage—In the root word *mile* the E is needed to make the I say its name. In this word the E is not dropped even though we are adding the vowel suffix *-age*.

Closeable, rideable, sizeable, microwaveable—In the root words *close, ride, size, and microwave* the E is needed to make the vowel say its name. In these words the E is not dropped even though we are adding the vowel suffix *-able*.

Type 2

Truly, duly, and **argument**—In base words *true, due,* and *argue* the silent final E is needed to prevent U from being at the end. In these words the E is dropped even though we are adding consonant suffixes to form *truly, duly,* and *argument*. The E is retained, however, according to the rule in the derivative *trueness*.

Type 4

Acreage—The root word *acre* has a silent final E because every syllable must have a vowel. In this case, the silent final E is retained because the suffix *-age* forms a new syllable and would leave the second syllable of *a cre age* without a vowel. This is the only known word where the E is retained for the syllable.

Type 6

Awful—The root word *awe* has a silent E to add length to the word. The silent final E is dropped when adding the consonant suffix *-ful* to form *awful*. It is retained, however, in the derivative *awesome*.

Type 8

Sometimes the E is retained when adding a vowel suffix in order to clarify homophones.

Silent E Retained	Homophone
dye + ing → dyeing	die + ing → dying
singe + ing → singeing	sing + ing → singing

Other

Judgment, acknowledgment—The root words *judge* and *knowledge* both end
with the multi-letter phonogram dge . Nevertheless, in standard American
spelling the E is dropped when adding the consonant suffix *-ment*. The E is
retained in the standard British spellings *judgement* and *acknowledgement*.

Not So Silent Final E's

Although we do sound the E in a few one-syllable words and a limited number
of multisyllable words, most final E's are silent. The following list includes all
the known words where the final E is heard. Each of these words follows the
rule: A, E, O, U usually say their name at the end of the syllable.

me	he	she	we
be	the*	apostrophe	acne
catastrophe	epitome	kamikaze	karate
recipe	coyote	simile	adobe

Learning all the reasons for silent final E's is one of the simplest ways to
improve spelling and reading skills. These rules can be taught quickly and provide a great deal of relief to students who are struggling. Though there are nine
reasons, the first four describe the majority of English words and are the most
vital for young students to learn. Knowing all the reasons greatly reduces frustration with decoding words. Adding suffixes to English words poses some of
the greatest difficulties for the spelling of more advanced words. Knowing why
the E is needed and whether it may be dropped is one of the most powerful
spelling tools you can give a student.

---

* The word *the* is pronounced /THə/ in daily speech. For spelling purposes we will exaggerate the
vowel sound to long /ē/. See Chapter 16: Overcoming Challenges: Creating an Auditory Picture.

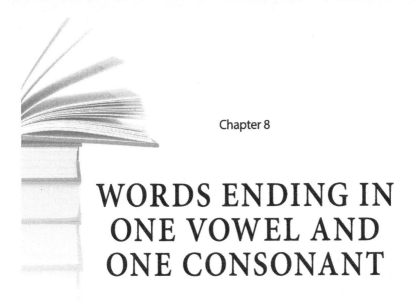

Chapter 8

WORDS ENDING IN ONE VOWEL AND ONE CONSONANT

A dding suffixes is a common area of confusion for many people. As we saw in Chapter 7, silent final E words change when adding a vowel suffix. Likewise, words ending in one vowel followed by one consonant change when adding a vowel suffix.

Most English writers recognize that consonants are doubled when adding suffixes to certain words. Some learned the rule "double the last consonant after a short vowel sound." This rule works for words like *hopping, tapping, forgetting,* and *referring,* but what about words such as *controlling* and *wainscotting* where the vowel sound is long? It also does not explain words such as *opening, medalist,* and *preference* which do not double the consonant after a short vowel sound.

In addition, many people confuse word pairs such as *hopping* and *hoping,* and *twined* and *twinned.* Many adult speakers not only struggle to spell these words but are also unable to accurately read them out of context. Much to their embarrassment, many writers choose the wrong one when using spell-checker.

Before exploring how to add suffixes to words ending in one vowel + one consonant, we must first learn about syllable stress. When I was in school, I did not understand why we learned about stressed syllables. Nevertheless, stress is foundational to both pronunciation and, as I will demonstrate shortly, spelling.

Stress Within Words

Many people struggle to hear syllable stress correctly. Is it TA ble or ta BLE? They think they cannot hear a difference.

Consider, however, the following sentences. In these words, the difference in stress is clear, for it is the difference in stress that distinguishes meaning.

Put the **ob'** ject on the table.   I ob **ject'** to that statement.

The **stressed syllable** is the one that is said a bit louder or more strongly than the others.

Before analyzing words for stress, try the following experiment. Place your hand under your chin. Then whisper "help." Now say "help" a bit more loudly. Then say it louder and louder until you are shouting. What happens to your mouth as you get louder? It opens wider, and the chin drops down farther.

This same principle can be used to locate the stressed syllable within a word. Because the stressed syllable is the loudest, the mouth opens the farthest to say the stressed syllable. Therefore, the easiest way to find the stressed syllable is to put your hand under your chin and say the word naturally. Use it in a sentence if needed. Feel on which syllable your chin drops down the farthest. That is the stressed syllable.

Find the stressed syllable in the following words. Place your hand under your chin and say each word naturally. Notice on which syllable the jaw drops open the farthest.

equip   cancel
offer   accent

The mouth drops open on the bold syllables: **equip, can**cel, **offer, ac**cent.

A second tip is that prefixes and suffixes are rarely stressed. Consider the following words. Feel the chin movement. The stress is on the base word.

return   resell
needed   singing

The stresses are as follows: re**turn,** re**sell, need**ed, **sing**ing.

One distinctive of English speech is that any vowel in an unstressed syllable may be pronounced as the schwa or /ə/ sound, whereas the vowel sound is clearly pronounced in the stressed syllable.

a bout'	ə bout
les' son	les sən

The **schwa** /ə/ is an unstressed vowel which sounds very similar to short U /ŭ/. Hold your hand under you chin and say /ə/. Then compare it to the other vowel sounds by saying: / ə ă ə ā ə ä ə ĕ ə ē ə ĭ ə ī ə ŏ ə ō ə oo ə ū/. You will notice your mouth drops open farther when pronouncing the other vowel sounds.

Knowing about schwa sounds is an aid to identifying the stressed syllable. To find the stressed syllable, locate the syllable with the clearly pronounced vowel. Feel your chin and listen for the clearly pronounced vowel sounds in the following words.

away	extra	pencil	button

The stresses are on the clearly pronounced vowels: a**way, ex**tra, **pen**cil, **but**ton.

Rule 14

We are now ready to explore the rule that controls how to add suffixes to words ending in one vowel + one consonant. Each part of the rule will be considered step by step. When understood, the rule explains how to add a suffix to words ending in one vowel followed by one consonant.

Admittedly, this is by far the most complicated rule presented in *Uncovering the Logic of English*. Do not let it bog you down. Glean what you are able to, and then continue reading through the book. If necessary, return to this chapter for further study after completing the book.

> **Rule 14**   Double the last consonant when adding a vowel suffix to
> words ending in **one vowel** followed by **one consonant**
> only if the syllable before the suffix is stressed.*
>
> *This is always true for one-syllable words.

One Vowel + One Consonant

Rule 14 only applies to words ending in **one** vowel + **one** consonant. Before introducing the questions which help us apply this rule, we need to understand the definition of one vowel + one consonant words.

Rule 14 only applies to words with **one vowel** that is seen and heard. This means only words using the single vowels $\boxed{a}$, $\boxed{e}$, $\boxed{i}$, $\boxed{o}$, $\boxed{u}$, $\boxed{y}$.

$$mad + en \rightarrow madden$$
$$let + ing \rightarrow letting$$
$$big + est \rightarrow biggest$$
$$stop + ing \rightarrow stopping$$
$$pup + y \rightarrow puppy$$
$$gyp + ed \rightarrow gypped$$

Rule 14 does not apply to base words ending with multi-letter vowel phonograms such as: $\boxed{ee}$, $\boxed{ea}$, $\boxed{ai}$, etc., followed by one consonant.

$$sleep + ing \rightarrow sleeping$$
$$treat + ed \rightarrow treated$$
$$restrain + ing \rightarrow restraining$$
$$appear + ance \rightarrow appearance$$

Double the last consonant only after **one consonant** that is **seen** and **heard**.

$$fad + ish \rightarrow faddish$$
$$pet + ing \rightarrow petting$$
$$sup + er \rightarrow supper$$

Do not double the last consonant if the word ends in more than one consonant.

pick +ing ➡ picking

sing + ing ➡ singing

arrest +ing ➡ arresting

comb +ed ➡ combed

Do not double the last consonant if the word ends in $\boxed{x}$. The phonogram $\boxed{x}$ represents two heard consonant sounds: /k/ and /s/.

tax + ing ➡ taxing

fix + ed ➡ fixed

relax + ing ➡ relaxing

The multi-letter phonogram $\boxed{qu}$ represents the sound /kw/. Q always needs a U; U is not a vowel here. Since the U is not a vowel but part of a multi-letter phonogram, double the last consonant before adding a vowel suffix if the word conforms to Rule 14.

quit +ing ➡ quitting

quiz + ed ➡ quizzed

Likewise the phonograms $\boxed{ow}$, $\boxed{aw}$, and $\boxed{ew}$ are multi-letter vowel phonograms. W is not a consonant in these phonograms, just as U is not a vowel in the phonogram $\boxed{qu}$. Therefore, do not double the last consonant when adding a vowel suffix.

show +ing ➡ showing

allow +ance ➡ allowance

saw + ing ➡ sawing

few + est ➡ fewest

The R-controlled phonograms, ar , er , ir , and ur , represent one distorted vowel sound followed by one consonant sound. Since one vowel and one consonant are both seen and heard, double the last consonant before adding a vowel suffix.

> star + ing → starring
> stir + ed → stirred
> blur + y → blurry

Questions

This rule leads us to two questions that must be asked when adding a suffix to one vowel + one consonant words:

> Are we adding a vowel suffix?
> Is the syllable before the suffix stressed?*
>
> *One-syllable words are always stressed.

If the answer to both questions is "yes," double the last consonant and add the suffix. If the answer to either question is "no," just add the suffix.

Are we adding a vowel suffix?

First, double the last consonant only when adding a **vowel** suffix. A vowel suffix is an ending that begins with a vowel. For example: -*able, -ing, -ed, -ish,* and -*y*. In contrast, a consonant suffix begins with a consonant. For example: -*ly, -ness, -ful, -hood,* and -*ment*. In the following examples, notice that the last consonant is not doubled when adding a consonant suffix.

> mad +ly → madly
> ship + ment → shipment
> com mit + ment → commitment
> for get + ful → forgetful
> e quip + ment → equipment

Is the syllable before the suffix stressed?

Second, in order to apply this rule correctly to all words, we must know which syllable is stressed. Double the last consonant only if the stress in the new derivative word is on the syllable before the suffix.

Carefully consider the following words using the questions for adding a suffix.

hop + ing ➞ **hop'** p̲ing

rob + er ➞ **rob'** b̲er

swim + er ➞ **swim'** m̲er

cut + ing ➞ **cut'** t̲ing

pin + ing ➞ **pin'** n̲ing

ship + ing ➞ **ship'** p̲ing

Are we adding a vowel suffix? "Yes." Is the stress on the syllable before the suffix? "Yes." Therefore, double the last consonant before adding the vowel suffix.

The syllable before the suffix is always stressed in one-syllable words. Therefore, the consonant is always doubled when adding a vowel suffix to one-syllable words ending in one vowel + one consonant. One way to simplify this rule for young students is to begin with one-syllable words and leave out the question of syllable stress.

In multisyllable words, on the other hand, it is vital to listen for (or feel)[*] the stress. Compare each of the pairs carefully. In the first word, the syllable before the suffix **is stressed**. Therefore, the consonant **is doubled**. In the second word, the syllable before the suffix is **not stressed**. Therefore, the consonant is **not doubled**.

1.   medal + ion ➞ me **dal'** l̲ion

2.   medal + ist ➞ **med'** al ist

---

[*] Some people find that feeling their chin for the stressed syllable is the most effective way to determine the stress for spelling.

1.   omit + ing ➺ o **mit'** ting

2.   limit + ing ➺ **lim'** it ing

1.   prefer + ing ➺ pre **fer'** ring

2.   prefer + ence ➺ **pref'** er ence

1.   confer + ing ➺ con **fer'** ring

2.   confer + ence ➺ **con'** fer ence

Consider the following examples. As you ask yourself the questions, I encourage you to take time to perform the chin test for each word and observe how the syllable stress affects the spelling.

forget + ing ➺ for **get'** ting

commit + ee ➺ com **mit'** tee

rebel + ion ➺ re **bel'** lion

begin + er ➺ be **gin'** ner

equip + ing ➺ e **quip'** ping

occur + ed ➺ oc **cur**red'

control + ing ➺ con **trol'** ling

Are we adding a vowel suffix? "Yes." Is the stress on the syllable before the suffix? "Yes." Then double the last consonant before adding the suffix.

Now we will consider words where the syllable before the suffix is not stressed.

profit +ing ➺ **pro'** fit ing

open +ing ➺ **o'** pen ing

offer +ed ➺ **of'** fered

alter + ed ➺ **al'** tered

prefer + ence ➺ **pref'** er ence

parallel + ed ➺ **par'** a leled

margin +al ➺ **mar'** gin al

cater +ing ➺ **ca'** ter ing

Are we adding a vowel suffix? "Yes." Is the stress on the syllable before the suffix? "No." Therefore, do not double the last consonant.

Take a moment to notice how many of the previous examples would be misspelled if the syllable stress were not considered. These are just a few of the thousands of words that are affected by syllable stress.

If you feel overwhelmed by Rule 14, continue on. All the rules that follow are much simpler. If you have mastered Rule 14, the rest will be easy.

True Exceptions

Excellent and **excellence**—These words are formed by adding the vowel suffixes -ent and -ence to the base word *excel*. Although the stress is not on the syllable -cel, the consonant is doubled in both **ex'** cel lent and **ex'** cel lence.

The suffixes -ic, -ify, and -ity—When adding the vowel suffixes -ic, -ify, and -ity to multisyllable words the consonant is not doubled, even if the stress is on the syllable before the suffix. A few examples of words in this category include: *magnetic, acidify, humidify, normality, brutality, electricity,* and *credibility.**

In England and Commonwealth countries words ending in L are commonly doubled even if the stress is not on the final syllable. For example: *dialling* and *signalling.* For more information see Appendix J.

One Vowel + One Consonant or Silent E?

Many people confuse one syllable + one consonant words and silent final E words after a suffix has been added. The difference should now be more apparent. In order to differentiate between the words, it is necessary to first consider the base word and determine if it is a silent final E word or a one vowel + one consonant word.

Silent Final E	*One Vowel + One Consonant*
hope + ing → hoping	hop + ing → hopping
cute + er → cuter	cut + er → cutter

---

* To participate in further discussion of this rule and its exceptions see www.LogicofEnglish.com/forum/

pine + ing → pining   pin + ing → pinning
robe + ed → robed   rob + ed → robbed
twine + ed → twined   twin + ed → twinned

Rule 14 is a complex but powerful spelling rule. Fully understanding when and why consonants are doubled resolves many exceptions and provides the tools to spell accurately. In its simplest forms, Rule 14 also delineates how to decode words such as *pining* and *pinning*. These word pairs, which are commonly confused by even proficient readers, are easily sorted out when the correct rules are known. Without learning the basic spelling rules, many people remain confused their entire lives, as the differences between these words are too slight to memorize by sight alone.

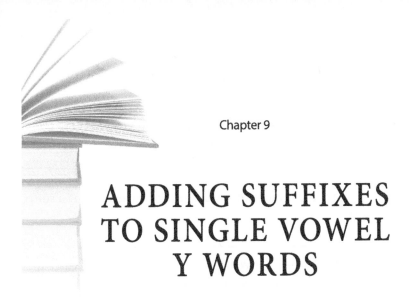

ADDING SUFFIXES TO SINGLE VOWEL Y WORDS

Words ending in single vowel Y are the final type of words that change when adding a suffix. The rule that governs words ending in Y is straightforward and easy to learn. It also explains some of the most frequently misspelled words such as *business*.[1]

As we have begun to show in Chapter 6, there is a deep relationship between I's and Y's in English. There are four ways in which I's and Y's are related. First, they share three vowel sounds /ĭ-ī-ē/ and one consonant sound /y/. Second, since English words do not end in I, Y stands in its place at the end of words. Third, there are multi-phonogram pairs ending in I or Y which may or may not be used at the end of words. Fourth, as most of us know, Y's change back to I's when adding suffixes.

Many English speakers feel confused about when the Y will change back to I. Others wonder why the Y remains in the words *applying* and *employs* but changes in *application* and *theories*. Here is a clear rule which explains when the Y changes to I.

> **Rule 15**   Single vowel Y changes to I when adding any ending,
> unless the ending begins with I.

This rule leads us to two questions that must be asked when adding a suffix to words ending in Y:

> Does it end with a single vowel Y?
> Does the suffix begin with any letter except I?

If the answer to both questions is "yes," change the Y to I and add the suffix. If the answer to either question is "no," just add the ending.

Does it end with a single vowel Y?

First, it is vital to understand that this rule only applies to a **single** vowel Y. The multi-letter phonograms oy , ay , and ey are two-letter vowels. The Y does not change to I when adding a suffix to words ending with a multi-letter phonogram.

Consider each of the following words.

boy + s ➙ boys	annoy + ed ➙ annoyed
stray + ed ➙ strayed	play + er ➙ player
survey + ed ➙ surveyed	attorney + s ➙ attorneys

Does it end with a single vowel Y? "No."

Does the suffix begin with any letter except I?

Using the questions for adding a suffix to words ending with Y, consider each of the following words.

busy + ness ➙ business	happy + ness ➙ happiness
try + es ➙ tries	puppy + es ➙ puppies

cry + er ➝ crier   baby + es ➝ babies

worry + some ➝ worrisome   salary + es ➝ salaries

ornery + est ➝ orneriest   cuddly + er ➝ cuddlier

Does "busy" end with a single vowel Y? "Yes." Does the suffix begin with any letter except I? "Yes." Therefore, change the Y to I before adding the suffix.

Since English words do not end in I, Y acts as a stand-in for I at the end of the word. When a suffix is added, the I is no longer at the end. Therefore, the Y changes back to I. This occurs with any ending, unless the ending begins with I, because:

Rule 16   Two I's cannot be next to one another in English words.

With this in mind, consider the following examples:

study +ing ➝ studying   clarify +ing ➝ clarifying

cry +ing ➝ crying   baby +ish ➝ babyish

worry + ing ➝ worrying   simplify + ing ➝ simplifying

Does it end with a single vowel Y? "Yes." Does the suffix begin with any letter except I? "No." Therefore, keep the Y before adding the suffix.

Exceptions

Single syllable words ending in a single vowel Y present the greatest number of exceptions to a Logic of English spelling rule. However, put into perspective, there are only fourteen words formed from seven base words which are exceptions. Of the thousands of words ending in Y these still represent less than 1%.

Buyable, buyer, dryness, flyable, shyer, shyly, shyness, slyness, slyer, slyest, spryly, spryness, wryness, wryly—Each of these one-syllable words retains the Y when according to Rule 15 it should be changed to I. It should be noted that all of these are one-syllable words where the Y is saying the long /ī/ sound at the end of the base word.

There are also eleven words in English where both spellings are accepted.

drier	dryer
drily	dryly
dries	drys
flier	flyer
frier	fryer
shiest	shyest
slily	slyly
sprier	spryer
spriest	spryest
wrier	wryer
wriest	wryest

Skiing, radii, Hawaii, and **Hawaiian**—A few foreign words have two I's next to one another. Ski is a Norwegian word that ends in I. Just add the suffix -*ing* to form *skiing*. Other commonly known words with a double I are *radii*, the Latin plural of radius, *Hawaii*, and *Hawaiian*.

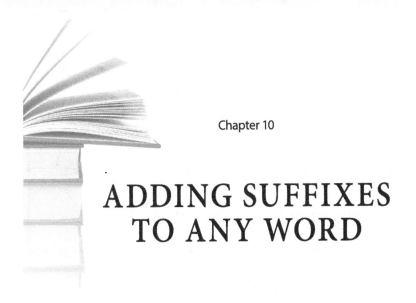

Chapter 10

ADDING SUFFIXES TO ANY WORD

S urely one of the most confusing aspects of English spelling is adding suffixes. However, in *Uncovering the Logic of English*, you have discovered there is a system which explains 98% of English words. The trick is to categorize the base words and to know which questions to ask for each type.

The flow chart on the next page is an excellent reference guide for adding suffixes. This tool will direct you as to which rules to apply to various words when adding an ending.

To add a suffix to any word, first ask the three questions in the first box. If the answers are all "no," just add the suffix. If the answer to any of the questions is "yes," continue by asking the questions for that type of word.

This is a useful tool for students to have handy in their notebooks or next to their computers.

Adding a Suffix to Any Word

Does it end with a **Silent Final E**?
Does it end with **One Vowel + One Consonant** (seen and heard)?
Does it end with a **Y**?

If **yes,** continue with the questions for the word type below.
If **no**, just add the suffix.

Silent Final E

Are we adding a vowel suffix?
Is dropping the E allowed by other spelling rules?
C says /s/ before E, I, and Y.
G may say /j/ before E, I, and Y.
If **yes,** drop the E and add the suffix.
If **no**, retain the E and add the suffix.

One Vowel + One Consonant

Are we adding a vowel suffix?
Is the syllable before the suffix stressed?
If **yes**, double the last consonant and add the suffix.
If **no**, just add the suffix.

Single Vowel Y

Does the word end with a single vowel Y?
Does the suffix begin with any letter except I?

If **yes**, change the Y to I and add the suffix.
If **no**, retain the Y and add the suffix.

Let's practice adding suffixes using the steps shown on the previous page.

travel + ed

Does it end with a Silent Final E? No.

Does it end with One Vowel + One Consonant? Yes.

Are we adding a vowel suffix? Yes.

Is the syllable before the suffix stressed? No. The stress is on the first syllable: trav' eled

Then just add the suffix to spell: traveled.

temporary + ly

Does it end with a Silent Final E? No.

Does it end with One Vowel + One Consonant? No.

Does it end with a Y? Yes.

Does it end with a single vowel Y? Yes.

Does the suffix begin with any letter except I? Yes.

Then change the Y to I and add the suffix to spell: temporarily.

behave + ing

Does it end with a Silent Final E? Yes.

Are we adding a vowel suffix? Yes.

Is dropping the E allowed by other spelling rules? Yes. The E is not needed for a C or G.

Then drop the E and add the suffix to spell: behaving.

courage + ous

Does it end with a Silent Final E? Yes.

Are we adding a vowel suffix? Yes.

Is dropping the E allowed by other spelling rules? No. G may say /j/ only before an E, I, or Y.

Then retain the E and add the suffix to spell: courageous.

support + ed

Does it end with a Silent Final E? No.
Does it end with One Vowel + One Consonant? No.
Does it end with a Y? No.

Then just add the suffix to spell: supported.

oblige + ation

Does it end with a Silent Final E? Yes.
Are we adding a vowel suffix? Yes.
Is dropping the E allowed by other spelling rules? Yes, the G changes its
    pronunciation to the hard sound /g/ in the derivative.

Then drop the E and add the suffix to spell: obligation.

control + ing

Does it end with a Silent Final E? No.
Does it end with One Vowel + One Consonant? Yes.
Are we adding a vowel suffix? Yes.
Is the syllable before the suffix stressed? Yes. con trol' ing

Then double the last consonant and add the suffix to spell: controlling.

employ + ment

Does it end with a Silent Final E? No.
Does it end with One Vowel + One Consonant? No.
Does it end with a Y? Yes.
Does it end with a single vowel Y? No.

Then retain the Y and add the suffix to spell: employment.

Chapter 11

THE POWER OF THE LATIN SPELLINGS OF /SH/

The three Latin spellings of /sh/, ti , ci , and si , are some of the most powerful phonograms for reading and spelling. Many students begin to plateau in their reading levels after learning to read simple one- and two-syllable words. Yet knowing these three phonograms helps to unlock the mystery of thousands of multisyllable words.

The Latin spellings of /sh/ also expose an area where most English students are taught a gross oversimplification: most students learn only the ending *-tion*. Many programs teach the ending *-tion* by showing a pattern of words such as *exception, addiction, promotion, repetition, prohibition,* etc. These programs conveniently leave out words such as:

dieti**tian**	physi**cian**	confes**sion**	divi**sion**
par**tial**	fa**cial**	reces**sion**	transfu**sion**

These words sound the same but are spelled differently. This sort of teaching gives an oversimplistic impression of the language and breeds confusion, whereas knowing that the phonograms ti , ci , and si each say /sh/ greatly simplifies decoding.

The Latin spellings of /sh/, [ti], [ci], and [si], are frequently found in advanced words in the English lexicon. They commonly appear with the seven suffixes shown in the chart below.

Table 9:   Suffixes Used with the Latin Spellings

	ti	*ci*	*si*
-al	torrential	commercial	controversial
-an	Egyptian	clinician	Russian
-ary	penitentiary	judiciary	
-ate	negotiate	appreciate	prussiate
-ent	quotient	sufficient	
-on	exception	coercion	recession
-ous	cautious	delicious	

It is also important to know that [si] represents a voice/unvoiced pair: the unvoiced /sh/ as in recession and the voiced /ZH/ as in division.

The Latin spellings of /sh/ are one of the most valuable spelling tools. We can often determine which Latin spelling of /sh/ will be used in a particular word by considering the root word. Study the words in the following charts. The patterns are amazing.

Notice that when a root word ends in [t], the phonogram [ti] is formed in the derivatives. The parallel occurs in words ending in [c] where the phonogram [ci] is formed and words ending in [s], which form the [si] phonogram in the derivatives.

Table 10: Latin Roots Using TI

elect + ion → election

confident + ial → confidential

Egypt + ian → Egyptian

penitent + iary → penitentiary

different + iate → differentiate

quote + ient → quotient

infect + ious → infectious

Table 11: Latin Roots Using CI

race + ial → racial

physic + ian → physician

office + iary → officiary

suffice + ient → sufficient

face + ial → facial

Table 12: Latin Roots Using SI

discuss + ion → discussion

controversy + al → controversial

progress + ion → progression

manse + ion → mansion

Once English speakers give up on the fallacy that English is illogical and begin to notice the patterns in English, they will begin to develop strategies that aid in understanding the language instead of simply memorizing individual words.

Analyze the following words and see if you can determine why the **voiced** form /ZH/ is heard in each. Hint: the reason is consistent in all the words.

Table 13: Latin Roots Using the Voiced Sound of SI

divide + ion → division

explode + ion → explosion

allude + ion → allusion

conclude + ion → conclusion

diffuse + ion → diffusion

fuse + ion → fusion

The voiced form is heard in each of the words because each of the roots ends with the voiced consonant sound /d/ or /z/. The voiced sound carries into the voiced /ZH/. All roots ending in the phonogram $\boxed{d}$ will use the Latin spelling $\boxed{si}$ and are pronounced with the voiced /ZH/.

The Latin spellings of /sh/ are restricted by the following rule:

Rule 17   TI, CI, and SI are used only at the beginning of any syllable after the first one.

con trac **tion**   so **cial**   ten **sion**

The Latin spellings of /sh/ are used only at the beginning of a syllable after the first one. In other words, they may **not** be used at the beginning of the word or at the end of a syllable.

The phonogram $\boxed{sh}$ is the most frequent spelling of the sound /sh/ at the beginning of the word or the end of the syllable. Since the phonogram $\boxed{sh}$ is so common in high frequency words, this phonogram is readily taught in schools. Most students, however, do not know it is restricted by the following rule:

> **Rule 18** SH spells /sh/ at the beginning of a base word and at the end of the syllable. SH never spells /sh/ at the beginning of any syllable after the first one, except for the ending *-ship*.

Though this rule appears long and complicated, when broken into its individual parts, it is rather simple.

SH spells /sh/ at the beginning of a base word,

she	sheep
share	sheik

at the end of the syllable,

fish	pub lish
fin ish	ac comp lish

and in the ending *-ship*.

fellow ship	hard ship
friend ship	as sis tant ship

SH never spells /sh/ at the beginning of any syllable after the first one, except for the ending *-ship*.

Remember, it is the three Latin spellings of /sh/, ti , ci , and si , that spell /sh/ at the beginning of syllables after the first one.

CH says /sh/

The French spelling of /sh/, ch , is another example where many students are taught an oversimplification of English. Since the sound /ch/ is heard most frequently (in 382 words according to *The ABC's and All Their Tricks*[1]), many phonics programs only teach the first phonogram sound /ch/.

cheese   chicken   chair

The second sound /k/ is heard in 146 Greek-based words.[2] For example:

orchid   stomach   epoch

The French spelling for /sh/, ☐ ch ☐, is found in 40 English words.[3] These words are not exceptions but a common pattern in English.

machine   cliche   crochet   mustache
chagrin   chaperone   champagne   chef
Chicago   parachute   chenille   chandelier

Students need to learn that ☐ ch ☐ represents three sounds /ch-k-sh/

True Exceptions

When considering how many thousands of words conform to the /sh/ rules, it is refreshing to know there are only three common exceptions.

Mar **sh**al and ban **sh**ee are rare occurrences of SH spelling /sh/ at the beginning of a syllable, after the first one.

Space which ends in a C uses the TI phonogram to spell the derivative *spatial*. This is because it is derived from the Latin root, *spatium*.

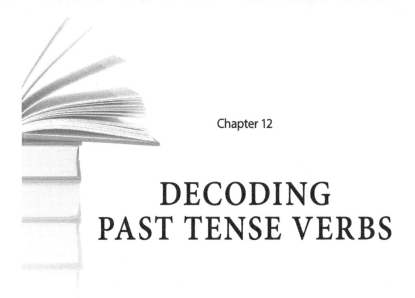

Chapter 12

DECODING
PAST TENSE VERBS

E nglish has a wonderfully simple way to form the past tense. Simply add the past tense ending ed . This is summarized by the rule:

> **Rule 19** To make a verb past tense, add the ending -ED unless it is an irregular verb.

The past tense ending ed says three sounds: /ĕd-d-t/. Recently, I was listening to an emerging reader sound out the word *cooked*. She read, "Cook Ed?" She looked very confused. Fortunately, knowing the three sounds of ed and why the variations exist provides a clear understanding of what is occurring and how to read past tense words. The same is true with spelling. To spell the word *matched* accurately, the writer must understand that this is the past tense form and that though /t/ is heard, it is spelled with the past tense ending ed .

The sounds of ed , /ĕd-d-t/, vary depending upon the final sound heard in the base word. Due to its high frequency, as well as the fact that it has three sounds, ed is best learned and memorized as a phonogram.

It is possible to discover which sound will be heard in a word by analyzing the patterns. Examine the words below. What is similar between each of the roots that causes the ed to be pronounced /ĕd/?

	ed	ed [2]	ed [3]
hand	hand **ed**		
demand	de mand **ed**		
land	land **ed**		
herd	herd **ed**		

Each of the words ends with /d/. Since it is impossible to clearly say /hănd-d/, the vowel sound /ĕ/ is inserted. This prevents the tongue from tripping and ensures the past tense ending is clearly heard in speech. As a result of the added /ĕ/ sound, a second syllable is formed.

Look at the next group of words. What is the pattern?

	ed	ed [2]	ed [3]
count	count **ed**		
support	sup port **ed**		
plant	plant **ed**		
digest	di gest **ed**		

Each of the words ends in /t/. Once again our tongues would trip over the sounds /t-d/ next to one another. Therefore the vowel /ĕ/ is inserted and another syllable is heard.

This next group is a bit trickier. See if you can find the pattern. All the roots have something in common so that $\boxed{\text{ed}}$, past tense ending, says /d/.

	ed	ed [2]	e d [3]
play		play**ed** [2]	
storm		storm**ed** [2]	
excuse		excus**ed** [2]	
owe		ow**ed** [2]	
perceive		perceiv**ed** [2]	

Each of these words ends in a voiced sound, and therefore, /d/, the voiced sound, is used when pronouncing the past tense ending. Since /d/ is easily and clearly articulated after each of these endings, the vowel sound /ĕ/ is not needed.

Find the common factor between each of the base words causing $\boxed{\text{ed}}$ to say its third sound /t/.

	ed	$\overset{2}{\text{ed}}$	$\overset{3}{\text{ed}}$
stamp			stamp$\overset{3}{\text{ed}}$
match			match$\overset{3}{\text{ed}}$
finance			financ$\overset{3}{\text{ed}}$
thank			thank$\overset{3}{\text{ed}}$

Each of these words ends with an unvoiced sound, therefore the unvoiced pronunciation /t/ is used. If you try to pronounce the voiced /d/ at the end of each word, you will notice it is difficult to switch from an unvoiced sound to the voiced /d/.

This is summarized by the following rule:

Rule 20   -ED, past tense ending, forms another syllable when the base word ends in /d/ or /t/. Otherwise, -ED says /d/ or /t/.

Exceptions

There are no known exceptions to the pronunciation of the past tense ending $\boxed{\text{ed}}$ described in Rule 20. Many people, however, claim irregular verbs are exceptions to forming the past tense. They often use irregular verbs as an example to prove how crazy the English language is. We have all heard jokes such as "If today I dive and yesterday I dove, why is it not, today I live and yesterday I love?"

English is not alone in its plethora of irregular verbs. According to one source, English has 178 irregular verbs, whereas Modern Greek has over 500, Italian over 400, Icelandic 350.[1] Memorizing irregular verb forms is a part of learning languages, particularly European languages.

Nevertheless, most of the irregular verbs in English follow patterns. Knowing how to analyze language by looking for patterns and understanding the phonograms and rules greatly simplifies memorizing irregular verbs. We will consider six variations of irregular verbs below.

(1) Many irregular verbs do not change in the past or participle form.

Present	*Simple Past*	*Past Participle*
bet	bet	bet
burst	burst	burst
cast	cast	cast
cost	cost	cost
put	put	put
quit	quit	quit

(2) Others change the spelling of a two-letter vowel to an O with a silent final E in the simple past tense, and add an -N to that for the participle.

Present	*Simple Past*	*Past Participle*
break	broke	broken
choose	chose	chosen
cleave	clove	cloven
freeze	froze	frozen
steal	stole	stolen

(3) Verbs containing the phonogram ‌ee‌ often change to the phonogram ‌e‌ in the past and participle forms.

Present	Simple Past	Past Participle
bleed	bled	bled
breed	bred	bred
feed	fed	fed
flee	fled	fled
meet	met	met

(4) A limited number of verbs ending in $\boxed{p}$ are spelled with the added phonogram $\boxed{t}$ in the past and participle forms

Present	Simple Past	Past Participle
creep	crept	crept
sweep	swept	swept
sleep	slept	slept
leap	leapt	leapt
keep	kept	kept
weep	wept	wept

(5) Verbs ending with the multi-letter phonogram $\boxed{ay}$, that **may** be used at the end of English words, change into two-letter $\boxed{ai}$, that **may not** be used at the end of English words. To put it another way, when $\boxed{ay}$ is no longer at the end of the word, the Y changes back to an I to form $\boxed{ai}$.

Present	Simple Past	Past Participle
pay	paid	paid
lay	laid	laid
say	said*	said*
slay	slain	slain
lie	lay	lain

---

* The word pair "say" and "said" is an example of the morpho-phonemic nature of English. In order to preserve the relationship in meaning, the common irregular verb pattern AY/AI is followed. Exaggerating the pronunciation as /sād/ will aid auditory learners in remembering the correct spelling. See Chapter 16.

(6) A limited number of verbs change from the phonogram ⟨ i ⟩ in the present tense to ⟨ a ⟩ in the past tense and ⟨ u ⟩ in the participle.

Present	Simple Past	Past Participle
begin	began	begun
cling	clang	clung
sing	sang	sung
drink	drank	drunk
shrink	shrank	shrunk

A list of irregular verbs is found in Appendix G.

Chapter 13

FORMING PLURAL NOUNS AND SINGULAR VERBS

Forming Plural Nouns

Just as there is logic to the past tense and its variations in pronunciation, there is logic to forming plurals and adding -*s* versus -*es*. The following rule is lyrical, teaches the spelling variation of the plural ending, and accounts for irregular English plurals. It is important when phrasing rules to alert students if there are irregularities to the language so as to not set up false expectations. Rules are to provide clarity, not to enhance confusion.

> **Rule 21**   To make a noun plural, add the ending -S, unless the word hisses or changes; then add -ES. Some nouns have no change or an irregular spelling.

Let's step through each part of this rule.

Just add -S

The most common way to make a noun plural is by adding the ending -S.

sons   banks   chairs   emotions

Remember the phonogram s makes two sounds: /s/ and /z/.

Hisses

Say the sounds: /ch/, /s/, /sh/, /x/, and /z/. Notice that each of these sounds hisses as it ends. When a word ends in a sound that hisses, add -ES to form the plural. Try to pronounce each of the words below by adding the /s/ or /z/ sound for the plural without the additional vowel /ĕ/.

watches   glasses

taxes   quizzes

pushes

It is impossible to clearly articulate another /s/ or /z/ sound at the end of a word that hisses. Therefore, the vowel sound /ĕ/ is inserted to ease articulation and ensure that the plural ending is clearly heard in speech.

Changes

When the root word changes to form the plural, add -ES. This is true for words where the Y changes to I.

puppy + es ➜ puppies   baby + es ➜ babies
pony + es ➜ ponies   story + es ➜ stories

In addition, some singular words that end with F change to V in the plural. When F changes to V, add -ES to form the plural.

thief + es ➜ thieves   knife + es ➜ knives
wolf + es ➜ wolves   shelf + es ➜ shelves

No Change

Before we talk about nouns which do not change in the plural form, we need to distinguish the two categories of English nouns: count and non-count nouns. The difference is determined by asking a simple question: can this noun be counted? If it is a person, place, thing, or idea that can be counted or tallied, it is a count noun and has a plural form. For example, it is possible to count the number of teachers, parks, tables, and holidays. Each of these nouns, therefore, has a plural form.

A non-count noun cannot be counted. Many non-count nouns are ideas such as friendship, mathematics, and poetry. Other non-count nouns are too numerous to be counted individually and therefore are measured in standard units such as inches, degrees, and pounds. Examples include cloth, heat, sugar, and gold. Others are typically not counted or measured such as hair and dust. Non-count nouns do not have a plural form and take a singular verb in sentences.

The sugar **is** in the cupboard.
Mathematics **is** my favorite subject.
My hair **flies** into my face in the wind.

When Rule 21 states: *Some nouns have no change . . .* it is referring to count nouns which do not change between the singular and plural form.

cod	perch	trout
walleye	tuna	shrimp
moose	sheep	bison
swine	aircraft	cannon
series	species	kiwi

These nouns can be either singular or plural in a sentence. The number is determined by any associated adjective or by the verb form.

I saw **one** deer in my backyard.
The deer **is** eating my garden.

I saw **many** deer in my backyard.

The deer **are** eating my garden.

Irregular Spelling

Many nouns have irregular spellings which reflect the original language. English, however, is not a static language. Over time many of the spellings have adapted to the English convention of adding -S to form the plurals. Many words now have both an irregular and a normalized English plural form. Both are accepted spellings.

Singular	*Plural*	*Normalized Spelling*
child	children	
formula	formulae	formulas
curriculum	curricula	curriculums

A more complete table of irregular plurals is included in Appendix H.

Forming Singular Verbs

English grammatical structure is relatively easy. Only the verb is conjugated to match the subject.

A plural subject takes the root form of the verb.

The boys play.

The dogs jump.

The third person singular is the only form that changes in English. (Third person refers to the pronouns *he*, *she*, and *it*.) This rule parallels the forming of plural nouns.

> **Rule 22** To make a verb 3rd person singular, add the ending -S, unless the word hisses or changes; then add -ES. Only four verbs are irregular.

Just add -S

The most common way to form a third person singular verb is by adding the ending -S.

He reads poetry.
She walks to school.
It falls off the tree.
The boy plays.
The dog jumps.

Hisses

The sounds /ch/, /s/, /sh/, /x/, and /z/ hiss. When a verb ends in a sound that hisses, add -ES to form the singular.

He boxes on Friday night.
She marches in the band.
It buzzes when I turn on the light.
The snake hisses.
The machine washes the clothes.

Changes

When the root verb changes to form the 3rd person singular, add -ES. This is true for silent final E words that drop the E, and for Y's that change to I.

live + es ➙ lives   Mary lives in Maine.
baby + es ➙ babies   Tom babies the dog.

In addition, a few verbs ending with F change to V in the 3rd person singular. When F changes to V, add -ES.

shelf + es → shelves   She shelves the books.

Irregular Spelling

Only four verbs have an irregular spelling in the present tense. Notice each of them ends with an -S in 3rd person singular.

1st Person Singular I	2nd Person Singular you	3rd Person Singular he, she, it	Plural we, they
have	have	has	have
do	do	does	do
go	go	goes	go
am	are	is	are

Chapter 14

CLEARING CONFUSION ABOUT AL- AND -FUL

S ome of the most commonly misspelled words involve the prefix *al-* and the suffix *-ful*. Many people misspell words with *al-* and *-ful* by writing two L's. The key to spelling these words correctly is to distinguish the words *all* and *full* from the prefix *al-* and the suffix *-ful*.

We will begin with the rules and then demonstrate how *al-* and *-ful* are acting as suffixes and prefixes in most words.

Rule 23	*Al-* is a prefix written with one L when preceding another syllable.

almost	also	always	although

Rule 24	*-Ful* is a suffix written with one L when added to another syllable.

truthful	regretful	eventful	useful

When *al-* and *-ful* are added to a base word, they are acting as a prefix and suffix.

Only suffixes change the spelling of the root word. Remember: single vowel Y changes to I when adding any ending unless the ending begins with I. Notice adding the suffix -*ful* causes a single vowel Y to change to I.

beauty + ful ➙ beautiful   mercy + ful ➙ merciful
bounty + ful ➙ bountiful

Contrast these examples with **compound words**. Compound words combine two or more *complete* base words to form a new word.

hand + bag ➙ handbag   hand + ball ➙ handball
hand + stand ➙ handstand   hand + writing ➙ handwriting

When forming compound words, the two base words do not change. They are simply written as one word without a space between them. Notice that the Y does not change to I when forming compound words.

body + work ➙ bodywork   any + one ➙ anyone
cry + baby ➙ crybaby

There are only three commonly known words where *all* and *full* are added to form compound words.

allspice   fullback   overfull

There are also four commonly used phrases which are written as two separate words.

all right*   all wrong   all day   all clear

---

* In formal writing, *all right* is spelled with two words. In dialogue and other informal writing the spelling *alright* is gaining acceptance.

Chapter 15

THE FINAL
SPELLING RULES

I n this chapter we will learn the final six spelling rules. Four of the rules limit the usage of the phonograms ⬚dge⬚, ⬚ck⬚, ⬚tch⬚, and ⬚z⬚. Another limits the usage and pronunciation of phonograms ending in GH. The final rule clarifies the spelling of many common words.

| **Rule 25** | DGE is used only after a single vowel which says its short (first) sound. |

ba**dge**	le**dge**	bri**dge**
lo**dge**	ju**dge**	

The phonogram ⬚dge⬚ may not be used after a consonant, a long vowel sound, a third vowel sound, or a multi-letter phonogram.

Since English words do not end in I, U, V, or J, ⬚dge⬚ is a common spelling of the sound /j/ at the end of words. The other commonly used spelling is G followed by a silent final E.

When the sound /j/ is heard at the end of the word and is preceded by a consonant or a long vowel sound, it is spelled G followed by a silent final E. See Chapter 7.

large	gorge	charge
rage	huge	age

Rule 26   CK is used only after a single vowel which says its short (first) sound.

back   neck   truck   lock et

The phonogram ⎡ ck ⎤ is limited in the same way as ⎡ dge ⎤. It may not be used after a consonant, long vowel sound, third vowel sound, or multi-letter phonogram.

Rule 27   TCH is used only after a single vowel which says its short or broad sound.

match	etch	glitch
splotch	hutch	

This rule varies from the previous two because in *watch* the phonogram ⎡ a ⎤ is saying its broad sound /ä/ and in *butcher* the phonogram ⎡ u ⎤ is saying its broad sound /ü/. The rule, therefore, draws the restriction around vowels near ⎡ tch ⎤ differently than Rules 25 and 26.

> **Rule 28** AUGH, EIGH, IGH, OUGH. Phonograms ending in GH are
> used only at the end of a base word or before the letter T.
> The GH is either silent or pronounced /f/.

Phonograms spelled with a GH are found only at the end of the word,

laugh   **weigh**   **sigh**   **tough**

and before the letter T.

caught   weight   night   bought

Words containing the letters GH originate in Old English. The GH was pronounced /kh/. In most modern English words the sound has been dropped; the GH is now silent.

tau**gh**t   ei**gh**t   fi**gh**t   fou**gh**t

In seven words the GH is pronounced /f/:

enou**gh**   rou**gh**   lau**gh**   drau**gh**t
cou**gh**   trou**gh**   tou**gh**

> **Rule 29** Z, never S, spells /z/ at the beginning of a base word.

zipper   zoo   zebra

It is helpful to realize [s] never spells /z/ at the beginning of a word.

Written Z's are rather uncommon in English, though they may occur anywhere within the word. There is no rule to indicate which spelling of the sound /z/ will be used in the middle or at the end of the word.

is	chairs	resist	wise
buzz	amaze	prize	enzyme

Knowing the phonograms and rules does not eliminate all memorization. Rather, they aid us in identifying which parts of words need careful attention. Words that contain the phonogram ⟨ z ⟩ in the middle or at the end are less common and will need additional thought and maybe practice.

> **Rule 30**   We often double F, L, and S after a single, short or broad vowel at the end of a base word. Occasionally other letters also are doubled.

off	ball	loss	ebb
odd	egg	inn	watt
jazz			

This rule is carefully worded to say we **often** double the letters. It is vital to not overstate rules and create unnecessary exceptions. Though the rule does not tell us when to double letters, it does cue the learner that F, L, and S are the most commonly doubled letters and to be aware that this occurs with other consonants as well. In addition, Rule 30 restricts doubling to after a single vowel at the end of the word. Final letters are not doubled after a multi-letter vowel or after a consonant.

reef	tool	famous	bulb

Occasionally other consonants are doubled as well. The lists below include all the commonly known base words which double a single consonant at the end of the word.

Table 14:   Base Words Ending in BB

ebb

Table 15:   Base Words Ending in DD

add	odd

Table 16:   Base Words Ending in GG

egg

Table 17:   Base Words Ending in NN

conn	inn

Table 18:   Base Words Ending in RR

err	burr	purr

Table 19:   Base Words Ending in TT

boycott	britt	butt
babbitt	mitt	watt
mutt	putt	

Table 20:   Base Words Ending in ZZ

buzz	fizz	frizz
fuzz	jazz	pizazz
razz	razzmatazz	schnozz
whizz		

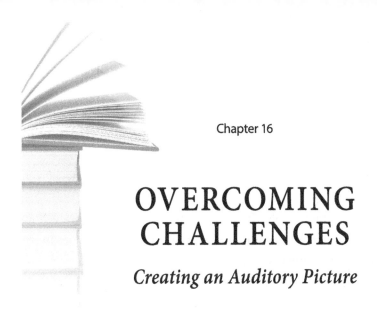

Chapter 16

OVERCOMING CHALLENGES

Creating an Auditory Picture

Most English-speaking students learn to read through a combination of memorizing sight words and a smattering of incomplete phonics. Spelling is then taught as a separate subject, rarely linked to reading. Yet reading and spelling are the same process in reverse. Reading is the process of decoding the "sound pictures" and reforming them into auditory words. This is true even when we are reading "silently" in our heads. Spelling is the process of hearing a word, breaking it into its individual sounds, and writing them on paper.

It is vital to understand that English is a code. Codes by nature are reversible. It is learning the keys to the code that enables all students to learn how to read and spell fluently. The key to reading and writing a phonetic language is the ability to break a word into its individual sound parts and to glue it back together.

In many languages there is a one-to-one correspondence between the phonograms (written symbols) and the phonemes (sounds). In such languages students at the end of first grade test at nearly the same level as college students in their ability to read and spell.[1] English, though, is a more opaque system where phonograms may represent more than one sound, and sounds may be spelled more than one way.

The primary solution to the difficulties presented by a complex code is to teach the code in its entirety and not to leave students guessing. Learning all the phonograms and spelling rules brings coherence in the midst of complexity.

Spoken English presents three additional problems: dialects, the schwa, and distortion of sounds.

These are not insurmountable. In this chapter I will demonstrate how pronouncing each word literally, as it is spelled, is a way to create an auditory picture of each word. All students of phonetic languages must learn how to exaggerate their pronunciation, though to varying degrees depending upon the language. This is because sounds are rarely found in their pure forms within words. Sounds in close proximity distort one another within the flow of natural speech.*

Let's first consider this process in regard to the problem of dialects.

Dialects

English is a global language with as many as 168 accents and dialects. Although speakers of each dialect usually can understand one another, there are distinctions which influence the pronunciation of various words. These variations in pronunciation are most distinct with the sound /r/ and vowels. Many speakers either add or drop /r/ sounds and morph vowel sounds based upon their dialect of English.

In the United States people in the Midwest pronounce the word *ten* /těn/. In the South the same word is commonly pronounced /tǐn/. If Southerners were to write *ten* exactly as they pronounce it, they would misspell it, *tin*. In addition, when reading, a young Southern student may not recognize /těn/ as the same word they commonly pronounce /tǐn/. To solve this problem we must teach all students to think /těn/ for purposes of reading and spelling.

This process is no different from the methods we use to auditorily recognize

---

* To solve this problem many written languages have characters that represent all the possible syllables. These writing systems are syllabic rather than phonetic. For English this would be impossible, since there are too many possible syllables. The number of possible syllables is very high in English due to the large number of vowels and consonant blends. Therefore a phonemic system, representing each sound, is the most efficient way to represent English words.

the speech of a person from another region. Just as we learn to hear words pronounced in other ways, we can learn to recognize that though the standard spelling may not represent our speech pattern, it does represent the speech pattern in some other region. Students should be explicitly taught these connections rather than left to discover them on their own.

Learning to pronounce words literally for spelling and reading purposes does not mean that students need to alter their daily pronunciation. Saying a word to spell and read is simply a tool to understand and memorize why a word is spelled in a particular manner.

Learning to pronounce the word for spelling purposes also heightens awareness of variations in pronunciation. After learning the phonograms, I became aware that my Canadian friend clearly pronounces the word *been* /bēn/, whereas I say /běn/. She does not need any additional tools to spell this word, for she says it exactly how it is written. I, however, teach my students to say /bēn/ for spelling purposes, thereby creating a clear auditory picture of the sounds.

Notice in the following chart how the standard British pronunciation clearly reflects the spelling of the vowels within each word. Recall that A, E, O, and U usually say their long sounds at the end of the syllable. For spelling purposes, Americans would benefit by learning to say each word as it is written.

	Standard American Pronunciation	Standard British Pronunciation
process	/prŏ sĕs/	/prō sĕs/
again	/ə gĕn/*	/ə gān/
been	/ bĕn/	/ bēn/

In contrast, many British speakers drop R's at the ends of words. They would benefit from exaggerating the /r/ sound for spelling purposes.

---

* We will discuss the schwa sound in the next section.

	Standard American Pronunciation	*Standard British Pronunciation*
father	/fäTH er/	/fäTH ə/
butter	/bŭt er/	/bŭt ə/
car	/car/	/cä/

In summary, spelling is best memorized by creating an auditory picture of how each word is spelled rather than relying on regional dialects and turning all variants from the dialect into sight words.

The Schwa

The schwa sound /ə/ is one of the distinctions of modern English speech. It is the most common spoken sound in both British and American English. The /ə/ is an essential part of the rhythmic patterns of English and is formed by unstressed syllables.

If you recall, we open our mouths most widely on the stressed syllable. This opening results in clearly articulated vowel sounds. The schwa is an unstressed vowel sound where the mouth is less open, and therefore, the vowel sound is less clear. The pronunciation of any English vowel may degrade to /ə/ in an unstressed syllable.

> **Rule 31** **Any vowel** may say one of the schwa sounds, /ŭ/ or /ĭ/, in an unstressed syllable or unstressed word.

Multisyllable words have stressed and unstressed syllable(s). In both American and British English most vowels in an unstressed syllable are pronounced /ə/. Consider the following examples:

We write	We say
con' stant	/kŏn' stənt/
trav' el	/trăv' əl/
cous' in	/kŭ' zən/
li' on	/lī' ən/
doc' tor	/dŏk' tər/
free' dom	/frē' dəm/
ig' no rance	/ĭg' nə rəns/

It is best to teach students to pronounce each syllable for spelling as if it were stressed. Exaggerating the pronunciation of words to create an auditory picture is a powerful tool to internalize correct spellings. It provides a system that is clear and rules that are consistent. Consider the following examples:

We write	We say	We say to spell
con' stant	/kŏn' stənt/	/kŏn' stănt/
trav' el	/trăv' əl/	/trăv' ĕl/
cous' in	/kŭ' zən/	/kŭ' zĭn/
li' on	/lī' ən/	/lī' ŏn/
doc' tor	/dŏk' tər/	/dŏk' tōr/
free' dom	/frē' dəm/	/frē' dŏm/
ig' no rance	/ĭg' nə rəns/	/ĭg' nō răns/

Another tool to determine the correct spelling of a vowel that is pronounced with a schwa is to find derivatives which have the stress placed on the desired syllable. Because English is a morpho-phonemic language where spellings are chosen to represent both sound and meaning, it is often possible to find a derivative where the vowel sound is clearly pronounced because the syllable is now stressed. Though this does not work for all words, it can be a simple way to clarify the spelling of a syllable with a schwa sound.

Unstressed	Stressed
və ca' tion	vā' cate
pə lit' i cal	pŏl' it ics
vi' təl	vi tăl' i ty
spə ci' fic	spē' cies
def' ə nite	de fīne'

Since words within a sentence also have varying amounts of stress, the schwa sound also occurs within short grammatical words. The important words, such as nouns, main verbs, adjectives, and adverbs, are stressed in speech. Therefore, their vowels are clearly articulated. The small grammar words such as articles, helping verbs, pronouns, and conjunctions are not stressed. As a result, the vowels within these words usually degrade into the schwa sound. Consider:

We write	We say
The man' sat'.	/THə măn săt./
a cup' of tea'	/ə kŭp ə tē/
what time'	/whət tīm/
She' was late'.	/shē wəs lāt./

It is beneficial to teach students to exaggerate the pronunciation of these words for spelling purposes. Just as with the issues related to dialects, it is important to make clear connections between what we say to spell and what we say in normal speech.

We write	We say	We say to spell
the	/THə/	/THē/
a	/ə/	/ā/
what	/whət/	/whät/
was	/wəz/	/wäz/

The lack of clear articulation of vowel sounds in unstressed syllables and words is a challenge for consistent spelling. Some people suggest that the schwa sound should be added to every vowel phonogram. This would provide no additional clarity for spelling. It would necessitate adding the schwa to every vowel phonogram, thus relegating virtually every multisyllable word to rote visual memory.

Students who are visual learners already learn to spell by memorizing how each word looks. If questioned on the spelling of a particular word, these learners will often write the word down to see if it looks right. They are relying on sight alone. However, reading and spelling are best taught using all of our learning modes: hearing, speaking, doing, and seeing.

When we use all the learning modes, the learning is deeper and faster. This is because each mode utilizes a different area of the brain. When all the areas are used simultaneously, we build synapses between the regions. Teaching by hearing, speaking, doing, and seeing also allows all students to utilize their strongest learning style while strengthening their areas of weakness.

Exaggerating the pronunciation of words for spelling adds the hearing and speaking modes. When this is combined with writing the words and logically analyzing the phonograms and spelling rules that are used, all students become more engaged and internalize spellings more quickly and deeply.

Distortion

Some sounds are distorted in the flow of natural speech by the proximity of other phonograms. This frequently occurs with sounds that are next to the vowel U. In order to clarify spelling, it is best to exaggerate the pronunciation.

Consider the word *sugar*. It has two syllables with the syllable break as follows: su gar. One would expect this word to be read /sū gär/. (U says /ū/ at the end of the syllable.) However, we say /shə ger/. To discover what is occurring within this word, pronounce the clearly articulated /sū gär/ faster and faster. You will notice the /sū/ naturally softens to /shə/.

Distortions occur because of the manner in which each sound is produced in the mouth and how we naturally change the sounds for ease of pronunciation. For spelling purposes, it is best to create a clear auditory picture of these words by exaggerating the pronunciation for spelling.

Conclusion

Most visual learners rely on memorizing the shape of individual words. This strategy, however, only works for students with strong visual memories. Therefore, it is best to teach students to create an auditory picture of each word as well. Students should be guided to clearly pronounce each vowel sound, enunciate /r/ sounds that are otherwise dropped, and articulate sounds that are distorted by close proximity to one another. When this is combined with writing, a kinesthetic experience of the word, all students' learning styles are covered, leading to faster and deeper learning.

Chapter 17

EFFICIENT SPELLING AND VOCABULARY DEVELOPMENT

High Frequency Words

Although English has a massive vocabulary, over 2 million words according to some counts, the 100 most frequently used words make up 50% of all that we read and write. The 300 most frequently used words make up 65% of all that we read and write. This is because a limited number of basic words are grammatically necessary to form all English sentences. These are the most essential. The first 300 comprise over half of every newspaper article, children's book, novel, or research article.

Table 21: Twenty Most Frequently Used Words

1. the	2. of	3. to	4. and
5. a	6. in	7. is	8. it
9. you	10. that	11. he	12. was
13. for	14. on	15. are	16. with
17. as	18. I	19. his	20. they

The first step to mastering English decoding and spelling is to begin by learning the phonograms and spelling rules within the context of high frequency words. In this manner students are learning the building blocks of all English words while at the same time mastering the words which are the building blocks to all sentences.

Developing a large vocabulary is the second most vital step to becoming a proficient reader and speller in English. It has been shown that many students who learn to read successfully in the lower grades plateau in fourth grade.[1] It is thought this is due to the rapid increase in volume and complexity of vocabulary. Fortunately, although the English lexicon is massive, a majority of words are formed either by combining words to form compound words or by adding suffixes or prefixes to roots.

Definitions

Before we continue, let's review and define a few terms:

A **prefix** is a group of letters added to the beginning of a root that alters the meaning.

A **suffix** is a group of letters added to the end of a root which alters the meaning or part of speech.

An **affix** is a group of letters added to either the beginning or ending of a word. There are two types of affixes in English: suffixes and prefixes.

A **base word** is a word that can stand alone when all the affixes have been removed. Let's consider the word *renew*. If we remove the prefix *re-* the base word *new* is left. *New* is a recognizable English word that stands alone, therefore it is a base word.

A **root** carries the primary meaning of the word but is not necessarily an English word when all the affixes have been removed. In the previous example, *new* is the root of the word *renew*. *New* stands alone, so it is also a base word. The word *revive* also has the prefix *re-*. Though *vive* is the root, *vive* is not a base word because it is not a recognizable English word. Roots which are not English words are sometimes call bound bases.

A **derivative** is a word formed by adding suffixes and prefixes to a root or by combining two base words to form a compound word.

Morphemes are the smallest word parts that carry meaning. Morphemes include roots, base words, suffixes, and prefixes. For example, the word *dogs* consists of two morphemes: the base word *dog* and the suffix *-s*.

Teaching Spelling and Vocabulary

Spelling and vocabulary development are ideally taught concurrently. Too often they are taught as independent subjects, cluttering the mind. When they are taught together, students build links between the roots and affixes and their spellings and meanings. Students also develop an increased awareness that English is a morpho-phonemic language where spellings represent both sound and meaning and begin to draw necessary connections between related words. In addition, teaching spelling and vocabulary at the same time aids students in developing reading fluency by teaching them to recognize not only the phonemes (parts of words that denote sound) but the morphemes (parts of words that carry meaning).

Too often we rely only on the context to provide clues to the meaning of an unknown word. Yet individual words contain vital information about their meaning.* When students are taught how to analyze a word based upon its roots and affixes, they are able to soar.

Consider the simple words: *love, forest,* and *view.*

love	forest	view
lovely	deforest	preview
loved	reforest	review
lovable	forestation	viewing
loveless	deforestation	reviewing
loving	reforestation	previewing
unlovely	forested	previewed
beloved	afforest	reviewed
unlovable		viewed
unloving		viewable

---

* This is an important argument for not drastically reforming English spelling. If we were to match each word to its pronunciation, words such as *sign* and *debt* would be spelled without the letters G and B. This would then diminish the connection to the cognates *signal* and *debit* where the sounds are clearly heard.

Each base word is a root which generates numerous related vocabulary entries. Adding suffixes and prefixes changes the meaning, tense, and part of speech. Simply learning the meanings of the affixes greatly simplifies the study of English.

For example, it is much simpler to learn *multi-* means "many" than to memorize each of the individual words: *multicultural, multidisciplinary, multi-faceted, multilingual, multilateral, multimillionaire,* and so forth. It helps even more to connect the prefix *multi-* to the commonly known words, *multiply* and *multiple.* Some students make these connections unaided. Since English is such a massive subject, however, many students never make the necessary connections when words are taught in isolation.

Students should begin to broaden their vocabulary as soon as they have mastered thirty to forty basic words. Vocabulary development follows in five basic steps.

Compound Words

First, learn how to read and spell compound words. A **compound word** is two words which are joined together to form a new word.

bed + room	➙	bedroom	mail + box	➙	mailbox
tooth + brush	➙	toothbrush	hand + stand	➙	handstand

Prefixes

Second, learn the most common prefixes and their meanings. Prefixes change the meaning of the root in one of three ways: they negate the meaning, intensify the meaning, or change the direction. Nine prefixes account for 75% of words that use a prefix. Twenty prefixes account for 97%.[2] It is wise to begin by learning the most commonly used prefixes before moving on to less common ones. A list of the twenty most common prefixes is included in Appendix I.

Table 22: 9 Most Common Prefixes

un-	not, opposite	undo, unhappy, unimportant
re-	again, back, against	redo, remix, return
in-, im-, ir-, il-	not, opposite	invisible, imperfect, irresponsible, illiterate
dis-	not, opposite	dislike, distaste, disloyal
en-, em-	to make, to put into, to cause	enact, encourage, encircle, encrust, enable, employ, emphasize, empathy
non-	not, opposite	nonthreatening, nonfiction, nonstop
in-, im-	within, in, into	inside, insight, invest
over-	much more than, too much	overdo, overstate, overload, overheat, overbearing, overcrowded
mis-	bad, wrong, not	misunderstand, misplace

Learning these nine prefixes and words that incorporate them is an efficient way to increase vocabulary. It is also a simple introduction to affixes as the base word remains unchanged.

un + pack → unpack

il+ legal → illegal

re + live → relive

mis + communication → miscommunication

Suffixes

Third, learn how to add suffixes to base words. Suffixes usually change the grammar of a word, make it singular or plural, change the tense, or alter the part of speech. Learning how to add suffixes is absolutely essential to mastering

English spelling. This is because silent final E, one vowel + one consonant, and single vowel Y words may change when adding a suffix. See Chapters 7–9.

communicate + ion ➺ communication
forget + ing ➺ forgetting
happy + ness ➺ happiness

Ten suffixes account for 85% of words that contain a suffix.[3] It is most efficient to begin with these before moving on to less common suffixes. For the 20 most common see Appendix I.

Table 23: 10 Most Common Suffixes

-s, -es	plural nouns, singular verbs	chairs, boxes, runs, walks
-ed	past tense	walked, climbed, lived
-ing	participle	walking, climbing, living
-ly	adverbs	lively, quickly
-er, -or	nouns; person or thing that does something	walker, climber, actor
-ion, -tion, -ation, -ition	forms nouns	fraction, starvation, translation, visitation
-ible, -able	forms adjectives, having the quality of	forcible, comfortable, dependable
-al, -ial	adjectives and nouns	comical, hysterical, perennial
-y	diminutives, adjectives, abstract nouns	daddy, chilly, jealousy
-ness	nouns, the quality of	happiness, restlessness

Multiple Affixes

Students are now ready to learn to identify the base word when more than one affix is added. The meaning of a word revolves around the root. Once students have identified the root and its meaning, they may then apply the meaning of the prefix.

unbendable = un + bend + able

The root is *bend*. The prefix *-un* means *not*. (*-able* forms the verb *bend* into an adjective.) *Unbendable* is an adjective describing something that cannot be bent.

previewed = pre + view + ed

The root is *view*. The prefix *pre-* means *before*. (*-ed* is the past tense ending.) *Previewed* denotes the action of having viewed something before the actual show or event.

Roots

Once students have mastered this process using base words, they are ready to apply their knowledge to roots. Remember, roots do not always stand alone as English words. Roots, especially Latin and Greek roots, are replete throughout English. Learning to recognize these roots and their meanings greatly reduces the amount of rote memory work for both spelling and vocabulary development.

A powerful example of an Old English root is found in the following words.

twin	twelve
twice	twelfth
twenty	two

Each of these words contains the root *tw*, meaning "two." Likewise, they all refer in some way to the number 2. Once students understand the root *tw*, they are not likely to mix up the homophone *two* with *to* and *too* and they will begin to understand how English spelling conventions reflect both sound and meaning.

Learning Latin and Greek roots is even more powerful than studying the English roots. Sixty percent of English vocabulary and 90% of scientific terminology is derived from Latin and Greek.[4] Ninety percent of all multi-syllable words are Latin based, and most of the remaining 10% are Greek based.[5] Each of these roots generates up to a dozen or more related words. It is extremely beneficial, therefore, for students to study vocabulary and spelling within the context of Latin and Greek roots.

Ideally, all teachers in the K-12 system would understand the logic of English and its value for teaching vocabulary. They would help students connect the vocabulary taught in their classes to other English words and to their roots. This should begin in the very earliest grades. For example, in an elementary math class, teachers should connect the base word *quart* with its meaning *fourth*. A quarter (25 cents) is a *fourth* of a dollar; a quart is a *fourth* of a gallon; a quarter (1/4) is a *fourth*; a quartet is *four* musicians.

A one- or two-minute vocabulary connection point would not only aid students in mastering a particular word but also reinforce how words are constructed in English and teach students to look for patterns.

Latin and Greek roots are the cornerstone of scientific vocabulary. Close to 100% of scientific terms have Latin or Greek roots. Understanding basic roots provides a context for learning the technical language of science outside of rote memorization. For example, the Latin term *ignus* means "fire." This should be connected to commonly used terms such as *ignition, ignite,* and *igniter*. With these connections it becomes clear that igneous rock was formed by fire or produced in molten lava.

A high school science teacher who is introducing the terms *exothermic* and *endothermic* should draw connections to other known words. *Therm-*, the Latin root for heat, is clearly related to words such as *thermal, thermometer,* and *thermostat*. *Exo-* is a prefix which means out. The teacher could point out that when a student *exits* the classroom they go out, an *exoskeleton* is one located outside the body, and something that *explodes* moves outward. Therefore an exothermic reaction is one that releases heat outward. The Latin prefix, *endo-,* means in. It is also found in the term *endoskeleton,* which is a skeleton located inside the body, and *endosperm*, food found inside a seed. An endothermic reaction thus absorbs heat or draws heat in.

A history teacher could aid students in understanding the *Acropolis* by showing students that *acro-* means heights as in an *acrobat* and *acrophobia*, and that *polis* means city as in *Minneapolis, Annapolis, Indianapolis,* and *metropolis*.

Consider the word *malicious*, commonly found on middle and high school vocabulary exercises. Usually it is embedded in a list of ten to fifteen unconnected words which students are asked to memorize for a vocabulary test later in the week. It only takes a few minutes to create mental hooks on which to hang the new term and thereby increase long-term retention for all learners. Students who are asked to find other words they know with the root *mal-* will usually state words such as *malfunction, maltreated, malformed* and *malnourished*. Since *malfunction* means to function badly, *maltreated* is treated badly, *malformed* is badly formed, etc., students will be able to deduce that *mal-* means "bad." These can also be connected to *maladjusted, dismal, malignant, malice, malefactor,* and *malady*.

By comparing *delicious, ambitious, gracious, spacious* and *suspicious* to *malicious*, students will notice that the suffix *-cious* means "full of something." They are then are able to deduce that *malicious* means "full of bad/evil."

Knowing roots also increases our understanding and appreciation for literature. This is true not only of the classics. Even contemporary writers often play with roots. The Harry Potter series is one example. Consider the character Malfoy. Knowing the meaning of the root *mal* provides insight into the character that may otherwise not be known. Understanding roots enriches good writing and enables us to more fully appreciate plays on words.

Examine the following examples. Consider how each word is related in meaning and spelling and how these relate to the root.

specto - to look at	*mot - to move*	*laboro - to work*
inspect	motion	laboratory
spectacles	motor	labor
spectacle	promote	collaborate

specto - to look at	*mot - to move*	*laboro - to work*
spectator	demote	elaborate
spectacular	locomotive	laborious
circumspect	motivation	laborer
respect	motive	lab

Each of the derivatives reflects the meaning of the root. Consider how knowing that *specto* means "to look at" unlocks the meaning to each of the derivatives. To *inspect* is to look at carefully. *Spectacles* are used to improve the eye's ability to look at things. When people make a *spectacle* of themselves, they become something to look at. A *spectator* is someone looking at an event. Something *spectacular* is something amazing to look at. *Circumspect* means looking carefully all around. To *respect* is to look on someone with regard.

This same reasoning can also be applied to *mot* and *laboro.*

The twenty most common prefixes and suffixes can also be added to Latin roots. Segmenting the word into its parts, it is possible to discover how words are constructed to convey meaning.

demote = de + mote

The root *mote* means "to move." The prefix *de-* means "down" as in *depress* and *devalue. Demote* therefore means "to move down." This is consistent with its usage: to move down in position or rank.

extract = ex + tract

The root *tract* means "to pull." The prefix *ex-* means "out." To *extract* means "to pull out."

destructive = de + struct + ive

The root *struct* means "to build." The prefix *de-* means "down." The suffix *-ive* connotes an adjective. *Destructive* describes something that builds down.

In addition to learning Greek and Latin roots, learning the meaning of common Latin and Greek prefixes can be a simple way to unlock the meaning to dozens of related words. It is more efficient to study the parts of words and how they work than to memorize each individual word. For example, *ambi-* is a Latin prefix meaning *both*.

ambidexterous	able to use both hands with ease.
ambiguous	having two or more possible meanings
ambitendency	having two conflicting tendencies
ambivalent	unable to decide between two choices of equal importance.

Roots are not limited to terms coined in the last century, either. Having an excellent command of roots, suffixes, and prefixes allows for great creativity in creating new words to describe inventions and discoveries. Xerox® is short for *xerography*, a word created to describe the new invention of "dry copying." *Xer-* is the Greek root for "dry" and *graphy* for "picture."

Conclusion

When students understand how words work, including phonograms, rules, roots, suffixes, and prefixes, they are prepared to read, spell, use words creatively, and communicate effectively. Though many intuitive students appear to absorb vocabulary by reading, other students need to be taught explicitly how to look for roots and compare them to other words they know. This basic vocabulary skill combined with learning the meanings of common roots and affixes will lead to a large and flexible vocabulary and the ability to use words with greater ease in comprehension, writing, and speaking.

Teaching words in isolation is the equivalent of teaching students to memorize number sentences such as "three plus two is five" without ever teaching them how to add. Students who learn how to analyze words will excel in their ability to master the technical vocabularies of science, medicine, and law. They are well prepared to comprehend and skillfully use the English language.

Chapter 18

PUTTING IT ALL TOGETHER

Learning the logic of English is important to solving our literacy crisis. The phonograms and rules presented in this book unlock the mystery of 98% of English words. As researchers have shown, systematically teaching the phonograms and rules ensures the success of all students. Unfortunately, the concepts in this book are not widely known among people who speak English. This has resulted in a literacy crisis which is affecting the entire fabric of our society.

Some people have tried to blame the problems on English. Admittedly, English is a complex code, though in this complexity lie powerful tools of expression, nuance, creativity, and meaning. It is essential when teaching English to lay out the system of the language explicitly so that all students can succeed.

English words are comprised of both phonograms (sound pictures) and morphemes (cues to the meaning). By learning the phonograms and rules that control their sounds, students acquire a strategy to sound out unknown words. By learning the morphemes, roots, suffixes, and prefixes, students grow better able to construe the meaning of unknown words. With these tools students no longer need to guess but have reliable strategies for reading and comprehending.

The phonograms, rules, roots, suffixes, and prefixes also contribute to success in spelling. With the advent of computerized spell-checkers, we have too often dismissed the importance of spelling, leaving countless people struggling.

Simply knowing the essential elements underlying each word informs writers. Though there remain some options for spelling, knowing the phonograms, rules, and roots greatly reduces the options and helps students identify which parts of words need more careful attention.

Currently, 69% of our nation's students are struggling with basic literacy skills. The material found in this book is vital to the next generation. Literacy is the foundation of our society—academically, civically, medically, environmentally, scientifically, and socially. Basic reading and writing skills should be taught in a manner that helps all students succeed. The logic underlying English should be known by everyone. When this information is combined with solid, multisensory teaching methods, we will experience a dramatic reversal in the literacy crisis.

If the material in *Uncovering the Logic of English* has changed your understanding of the English language, I encourage you to pass the book on to others. Together we can begin a grassroots movement that changes the lives of those who have suffered from illiteracy, and we can prevent it in future generations.

Sample Words to Tie It All Together

The purpose of learning the logic of English is to be able to analyze and understand any word within the English lexicon.

In this final chapter we will examine a few words using the phonograms, rules, and roots. Each word will be analyzed step by step. This process may be used by teachers to guide students in understanding words. In these examples, spelling is considered first and roots second. This order may be reversed depending upon the teaching context.

Though teaching in this manner initially means committing one to three minutes per word, the retention rate for meaning, pronunciation, and spelling will be much higher than if students are left to guess the spelling and meaning on their own. As students grow in their understanding of the logic of English, this time will shorten. Eventually, they will be able to analyze words almost instantaneously without assistance while reading.

homogeneous

1. *Divide it into syllables.*

   ho mo ge ne ous

2. *Analyze the word in the direction of reading and writing.*

   ho

   > O said /ō/ at the end of the syllable.
   > **Rule 4** A E O U usually say their names at the end of a syllable.

   ho **mo**

   > **Rule 4** as above.

   ho mo **ge**

   > G says its soft sound /j/ because of the E.
   > **Rule 2** G may say /j/ before E, I, or Y.

   > E said /ē/ at the end of the syllable.
   > **Rule 4** again.

   ho mo ge **ne**

   > E said /ē/ at the end of the syllable.
   > **Rule 4** as previous syllable.

   ho mo ge ne **o̱u̱s̱**

   > The multi-letter phonogram /ou-ō-ö-ŭ/ said its fourth
   > sound /ŭ/.

3. *Analyze the roots for meaning.*

   homo—**same**

   > Other words with this root include: *homophone* – words that
   > sound the same but have different meanings; *homogenize* – the
   > process of shaking milk so it does not separate, to make it the
   > same throughout.

gene—**family, kind, race**

Other words with this root include: *genealogy* – the study of families; *general* – applying to a whole class or kind; *generic* – an inclusive group or kind.

homogeneous—**of the same kind throughout.**

pedestrian

1. *Divide it into syllables.*

   pe des tri an

2. *Analyze the word in the direction of reading and writing.*

   pe

   Say to spell /ē/. E said /ē/ at the end of the syllable.
   Rule 4 A E O U usually say their names at the end of a syllable.

   pe **des**

   All first sounds.*

   pe des **tri**

   I is saying its third sound /ē/.
   Rule 7 I says /ē/ at the end of a syllable that is followed by a vowel.

   pe des tri **an**

   Say to spell /ăn/.
   All first sounds.

3. *Analyze the roots for meaning.*

   ped—**foot**

   Since the stress is on the second syllable, pe des' tri an, the first vowel is pronounced with a schwa sound /ə/. By listening to related roots, the vowel sound becomes clear as in *ped' dler.*

---

* Many phonograms make more than one sound. First sounds refer to the first sound as found in Appendix B.

Other words with this root include: *pedal* – something pushed with the foot; *peddler* – someone who goes from place to place selling, often by foot; *pedometer* – a device that measures the number of steps taken by foot; *pedestal* – the foot or bottom support of a column, pillar, or vase.

pedestrian—**a person traveling by foot.**

acceptable

1. *Divide it into syllables.*

   ac cept a ble

2. *Analyze the word in the direction of reading and writing.*

   ac c

   C says /k/ before another consonant.
   Rule 1 C softens to /s/ when followed by E, I, or Y. Otherwise, C says /k/.

   ac **cept**

   C says /s/ before an E.
   See **Rule 1** above.

   ac cept **a**

   Say to spell /ā/. A said /ā/ at the end of the syllable.
   Rule 4 A E O U usually say their names at the end of a syllable.

   ac cept a **ble**$_4$

   Rule 12.4 Every syllable must have a written vowel.

3. *Analyze the roots for spelling.*

   accept + able

   Does it end with a silent final E? No.
   Does it end with one vowel then one consonant? No. It ends with two consonants.
   Does it end with a single vowel Y? No.

   Then just add the suffix.

enlarging

1. *Divide it into syllables.*

   en larg ing

2. *Analyze the word in the direction of reading and writing.*

   en

   > All first sounds.

   en **larg** i

   > The multi-letter phonogram AR says /är/.
   > G says /j/ because of the I.
   > **Rule 2** G may soften to /j/ only when followed by E, I, or Y.
   > Otherwise, G says /g/.

   en larg **ing**

   > The phonogram NG says /ng/.

3. *Analyze the roots for spelling.*

   en + large + ing

   > Just add the prefix EN-.

   > *Does it end with a silent final E?* Yes.
   > *Are we adding a vowel suffix?* Yes.
   > *Is dropping the E allowed by other spelling rules?* Yes. The G will
   > still say /j/ before an I. See Rule 2 above.

   > Then drop the E and add the suffix.

4. *Analyze the roots for meaning.*

   large—**big**

   en—**to make into or to make like.**

   enlarging—**making bigger.**

acidic

1. *Divide it into syllables.*

   a cid ic

2. *Analyze the word in the direction of reading and writing.*

   a

   > Say to spell /ā/. A said /ā/ at the end of the syllable.
   >
   > **Rule 4** A E O U usually say their names at the end of a syllable.

   a **cid**

   > C says /s/ before an I.
   >
   > **Rule 1** C softens to /s/ when followed by E, I, or Y. Otherwise, C says /k/.

   a cid **ic**

   > C says /k/ at the end of the word.
   >
   > See **Rule 1** above.

mauve

1. *Divide it into syllables.*

   mauve

2. *Analyze the word in the direction of reading and writing.*

   mauve

   > The phonogram AU spells /ä/.
   >
   > English words do not end in V.
   >
   > **Rule 12.2** English words do not end in V or U.

confidential

1. *Divide it into syllables.*

    con fi den tial

2. *Analyze the word in the direction of reading and writing.*

    con

    All first sounds.

    con **fi**

    Rule 5 I and Y may say /ĭ/ or /ī/ at the end of a syllable.

    con fi **den**

    All first sounds.

    con fi den **<u>ti</u>al**

    TI says /sh/.

    Rule 17 TI, CI, and SI are used only at the beginning of any syllable after the first one.

3. *Analyze the roots for meaning.*

    con—**with**

    fid—**trust, believe**

    Other words with this root include: *fidelity* – faithfulness, trustworthiness to duties; *confident* – believing in oneself; *diffident* – not self-confident, not believing in oneself; *confide* – to trust someone and tell them about a private matter; *confidant* – a person trusted with secrets.

    confidential—**entrusted with secret or private matters.**

design

1. *Divide it into syllables.*

   de sign

2. *Analyze the word in the direction of reading and writing.*

   de

   > E says /ē/ at the end of the syllable.
   > **Rule 4** A E O U usually say their names at the end of a syllable.

   de **si͡gn**

   > S says its second sound /z/.
   >
   > I says /ī/.
   > **Rule 6** I and O may say /ī/ and /ō/ when followed by two consonants.
   >
   > The phonogram GN says /n/.

3. *Analyze the roots for meaning.*

   de—**out**

   sign—**mark**

   > Other words with this root include: *sign* – something that marks; *assign* – to mark out, to allot; *designate* – to specify, to mark out, to single out; *signal* – a sign.

   design—**to mark out plans, to make a plan.**

SPELLING RULES

Rule 1   C always softens to /s/ when followed by E, I, or Y. Otherwise, C says /k/.

Rule 2   G may soften to /j/ only when followed by E, I, or Y. Otherwise, G says /g/.

Rule 3   English words do not end in I, U, V, or J.

Rule 4   A E O U usually say their names at the end of a syllable.

Rule 5   I and Y may say /ĭ/ or /ī/ at the end of a syllable.

Rule 6   When a one-syllable word ends in a single vowel Y, it says /ī/.

Rule 7   Y says /ē/ only at the end of a multi-syllable word. I says /ē/ at the end of a syllable that is followed by a vowel and at the end of foreign words.

Rule 8   I and O may say /ī/ and /ō/ when followed by two consonants.

Rule 9   AY usually spells the sound /ā/ at the end of a base word.

Rule 10   When a word ends with the phonogram A, it says /ä/. A may also say /ä/ after a W or before an L.

Rule 11   Q always needs a U; therefore, U is not a vowel here.

Rule 12   Silent Final E Rules

    12.1   The vowel says its long sound because of the E.

    12.2   English words do not end in V or U.

    12.3   The C says /s/ and the G says /j/ because of the E.

    12.4   Every syllable must have a written vowel.

    12.5   Add an E to keep singular words that end in the letter S from looking plural.

    12.6   Add an E to make the word look bigger.

    12.7   TH says its voiced sound /TH/ because of the E.

    12.8   Add an E to clarify meaning.

    12.9   Unseen reason.

Rule 13   Drop the silent final E when adding a vowel suffix only if it is allowed by other spelling rules.

Rule 14 Double the last consonant when adding a vowel suffix to words ending in **one vowel** followed by **one consonant** only if the syllable before the suffix is stressed.*

*This is always true for one-syllable words.

Rule 15 Single vowel Y changes to I when adding any ending, unless the ending begins with I.

Rule 16 Two I's cannot be next to one another in English words.

Rule 17 TI, CI, and SI are used only at the beginning of any syllable after the first one.

Rule 18 SH spells /sh/ at the beginning of a base word and at the end of the syllable. SH never spells /sh/ at the beginning of any syllable after the first one, except for the ending -ship.

Rule 19 To make a verb past tense, add the ending -ED unless it is an irregular verb.

Rule 20 -ED, past tense ending, forms another syllable when the base word ends in /d/ or /t/. Otherwise, -ED says /d/ or /t/.

Rule 21 To make a noun plural, add the ending -S, unless the word hisses or changes; then add -ES. Some nouns have no change or an irregular spelling.

Rule 22 To make a verb 3rd person singular, add the ending -S, unless the word hisses or changes; then add -ES. Only four verbs are irregular.

Rule 23 Al- is a prefix written with one L when preceding another syllable.

Rule 24 -Ful is a suffix written with one L when added to another syllable.

Rule 25 DGE is used only after a single vowel which says its short (first) sound.

Rule 26 CK is used only after a single vowel which says its short (first) sound.

Rule 27 TCH is used only after a single vowel which says its short or broad sound.

Rule 28 AUGH, EIGH, IGH, OUGH. Phonograms ending in GH are used only at the end of a base word or before the letter T. The GH is either silent or pronounced /f/.

Rule 29 Z, never S, spells /z/ at the beginning of a base word.

Rule 30 We often double F, L, and S after a single, short or broad vowel at the end of a base word. Occasionally other letters also are doubled.

Rule 31 Any vowel may say one of the schwa sounds, /ŭ/ or /ĭ/, in an unstressed syllable or unstressed word.

BASIC PHONOGRAMS

The sounds for each phonogram are listed in order of frequency.

Phonogram	Sound	Sample Words		
a	/ă-ā-ä/	mat	table	father
ai	/ā/	laid		
ar	/är/	car		
au	/ä/	author		
augh	/ä-ăf/	taught	laugh	
aw	/ä/	saw		
ay	/ā/	play		
b	/b/	bat		
bu	/b/	buy		
c	/k-s/	cat	cent	
cei	/sē/	receive		
ch	/ch-k-sh/	child	school	chef
ci	/sh/	spacious		
ck	/k/	back		
d	/d/	dad		
dge	/j/	edge		
e	/ĕ-ē/	tent	be	
ea	/ē-ĕ-ā/	eat	bread	steak
ear	/er/	search		
ed	/ed-d-t/	traded	pulled	picked

Phonogram	Sound	Sample Words		
ee	/ē/	tree		
ei	/ā-ē-ī/	their	protein	feisty
eigh	/ā-ī/	eight	height	
er	/er/	her		
ew	/ö-ū/	flew	few	
ey	/ā-ē/	they	key	
f	/f/	foot		
g	/g-j/	big	gym	
gn	/n/	sign		
gu	/g-gw/	guide	language	
h	/h/	hat		
i	/ĭ-ī-ē-y/	it	ivy	stadium onion
ie	/ē/	field		
igh	/ī/	night		
ir	/er/	bird		
j	/j/	job		
k	/k/	kit		
kn	/n/	know		
l	/l/	lap		
m	/m/	me		
n	/n/	nut		
ng	/ng/	sing		
o	/ŏ-ō-ö/	on	go	do
oa	/ō/	coat		
oe	/ō-ö/	toe	shoe	
oi	/oi/	boil		
oo	/ö-ü-ō/	food	took	floor
or	/ōr/	lord		

Phonogram	Sound	Sample Words			
ou	/ow-ō-ö-ŭ-ü/	h**ou**se c**ou**ntry	s**ou**l c**ou**ld	gr**ou**p	
ough	/ŏ-ō-ö-ow-ŭf-ŏf/	th**ough**t b**ough**	th**ough** r**ough**	thr**ough** tr**ough**	
ow	/ow-ō/	pl**ow**	sn**ow**		
oy	/oi/	b**oy**			
p	/p/	**p**an			
ph	/f/	**ph**one			
qu	/kw/	**qu**een			
r	/r/	**r**an			
s	/s-z/	**s**ent	a**s**		
sh	/sh/	**sh**e			
si	/sh-zh/	se**si**on	divi**si**on		
t	/t/	**t**ip			
tch	/ch/	bu**tch**er			
th	/th-TH/	**th**in	**th**is		
ti	/sh/	par**ti**al			
u	/ŭ-ū-ö-ü/	**u**p	p**u**pil	fl**u**te	p**u**t
ui	/ö/	fr**ui**t			
ur	/er/	h**ur**ts			
v	/v/	**v**an			
w	/w/	**w**all			
wh	/wh/	**wh**isper			
wor	/wer/	**wor**m			
wr	/r/	**wr**ite			
x	/ks-z/	fo**x**	**x**ylophone		
y	/y-ĭ-ī-ē/	**y**ard	g**y**m	b**y**	bab**y**
z	/z/	**z**ip			

MORE ABOUT THE BASIC PHONOGRAMS

AUGH – says /ä/ in nine base words. It says its second sound, /ăf/, in only two base words. These words may be learned as a group.

ä	*ăf*
aught (more commonly spelled ought)	dr**augh**t
c**augh**t	l**augh**
d**augh**ter	
dist**raugh**t	
fr**augh**t	
h**augh**ty	
sl**augh**ter	
n**augh**ty	
t**augh**t	

CEI – Rather than learning the rule: "Use I before E, except after C . . . ," which has numerous exceptions, it is simpler to learn CEI as a phonogram. This phonogram is found in only eight common base words. These words may be taught as a group.

ceiling	con**cei**ve	re**cei**pt
de**cei**ve	per**cei**ve	re**cei**ve
con**cei**t	de**cei**t	

DGE – The sound /j/ heard in words such as *hedge* and *ledge* is harsher with more voice than the sound formed by G followed by a silent E as in *large* and *marriage*.

E – The single letter E spells the long /ē/ sound **at the end** of only six one-syllable words. Since Y says its long /ī/ sound at the end of a one-syllable word, as in *by, try,* and *fly,* the single vowel E is used instead.

he	she	we
the	me	be

Typically, Y spells the long /ē/ sound at the end of multisyllable words. There are eleven words, however, which are spelled with the single vowel E. These may be learned as a group.

acne	adobe	apostrophe	catastrophe
coyote	epitome	kamikaze	karate
recipe	sesame	simile	

EA – says /ā/ in only nine common words. These words may be taught as a group.

steak	break	tear
great	wear	pear
bear	swear	yea

EA spells the long /ē/ sound **at the end** of only six commonly used words. These may be taught as a group. (EA says long /ē/ in the middle of many words.)

flea	pea	plea
sea	tea	guinea

EAR – says /er/ in only thirteen commonly used base words.

earth	earn	heard
learn	early	earl
pearl	search	rehearse
dearth	hearse	yearn
earnest		

EE – spells the long /ē/ sound **at the end** of only thirteen commonly known base words.

bee	fee	flee	free
glee	knee	pee	see
spree	tee	thee	three
tree			

EI – The following lists include all the commonly known words spelled with the phonogram EI. Words such as deity and nuclei are not included because the E and I are acting as two separate phonograms as is seen by the syllable breaks: *de it y, nu cle i.*

The basic sounds were chosen because they are represented in common words such as *their, either* and *neither*. Since *either* and *neither* are also commonly pronounced with a long /ī/, and the relationship with EIGH is made more clear, I have chosen to include the long /ī/ as a basic phonogram sound.

Basic Phonogram Sounds

ā	*ē*	*ī*
beige	caffeine	apartheid
deign	casein	eider(down)
dreidel	codeine	Einstein
feign	either	(either)
feint	holstein	feisty

ā	*ē*	*ī*
geisha	leisure	fraulein
heir	neither	heist
lei	plebeian	kaleidoscope
reign	protein	(neither)
skein	seize	poltergeist
surveillance	sheik	rottweiler
their	Sheila	seismic
veil	weird	stein
vein		

Advanced Phonogram Sounds

ĭ	*ĕ*
counterfeit	heifer
foreign	
forfeit	
sovereign	
surfeit	

EIGH – is an uncommon spelling. It is found in only seven common base words. These words may be taught as a group.

ā	*ī*
eight	height
freight	sleight
sleigh	
weigh	
neighbor	

By adding suffixes and prefixes and using these to form compound words, these six words can be expanded into a total of 103 words.

EY – There are only ten commonly known words in which EY says long A. The long /ā/ sound is the least common sound. However, it is placed first because (1) memorizing the long /ā/ sound first helps to distinguish this phonogram from others and (2) it helps link this phonogram to EIGH and EI.

abeyance	convey	grey (British spelling for gray)
hey	obey	prey
purvey	survey	whey
they		

EY spells long /ē/ at the end of a single one-syllable word, *key*.
EY usually says its long /ē/ sound at the end of two- and three-syllable words.

abbey	attorney
chutney	baloney
hockey	

EY is a common suffix added to words to turn nouns into adjectives.

chocolate	chocolatey
glue	gluey

EW – says the long /ū/ sound where the /y/ is distinctly heard in only two base words: *few* and *new* (in some dialects). The rest drop the /y/ sound.

I – says the consonant sound /y/ in words such as *onion, opinion, union,* etc. Learning that I also has a consonant sound further emphasizes the I and Y relationship in English.

IE – Many programs (based upon 70 phonograms) have three sounds for this phonogram: /ē-ī-ĭ/. This program uses only one sound /ē/ for the following reasons:
Five common base words end in IE.

die	lie	pie
tie	vie	

These words are better classified as silent final E words because each of them drops the E when adding a vowel suffix. When adding the vowel suffix -*ed*, these words drop the E to form *lied, tied, died*. When adding the vowel suffix -*ing*, in addition to dropping the E, the I changes to Y to prevent two I's from being together. For example: *lying* and *dying*. Some teachers argue that the phonogram IE is formed when a single vowel Y changes to I when adding a suffix that begins with E. For example: *implied, tried*, and *cried*. From a pedagogical standpoint it is better to teach students to look at the root word and emphasize that the Y changed to I, rather than teaching these words as the phonogram IE.

IE says /ĭ/ in only two common words. Since these both in an unstressed syllable, we will "say to spell" long /ē/. This is also consistent with their root word, *chief*, and aids in emphasizing the morpho-phonemic aspects of English.

kerchief   mischief

IE spells long /ē/ at the end of a single one-syllable word: *brie*.
IE says /ĕ/ in only one commonly known word: *friend*.
IGH – is used in only nineteen common base words.

bight	blight	bright
fight	flight	fright
high	knight	light
might	nigh	night
plight	right	sigh
sight	slight	tight
thigh		

By adding suffixes and prefixes and using these to form compound words, these words can be expanded into a total of 720 words.

OA – is used in 62 commonly used base words. It is used in the middle of one-syllable base words with the exception of *approach, reproach, cocoa, quinoa*, and *whoa*. Words containing the phonogram OA commonly form compound words such as motorboat, toadstool, etc. They also commonly add prefixes and suffixes.

OE – is the least common spelling of the long /ō/ sound. There are only 9 common base words that use this spelling. These may be learned as a group.

doe	foe	hoe
oboe	toe	woe
aloe	roe	throe

OE represents a phonogram, not an O plus a silent final E. This is demonstrated by the E being retained when adding a vowel suffix in words such as *hoeing* and *toeing*. If it were a silent final E, the E would be dropped.

OE says its second sound /ö/ in only two common words.

shoe   canoe

OE is not acting as a silent final E in these words, as can be demonstrated by the fact that the E is retained when adding a vowel suffix such as *shoeing* and *canoeing*.

OO – By far the most common sound is /ö/. It is heard in more than 150 common base words. It says its second sound, /ü/, in twenty-one common base words and one suffix. It says its third sound, long /ō/, in only four base words. It says the short /ŭ/ sound in two words.

ü	ō	ŭ
the suffix -hood	boor	blood
book	brooch	flood
brook	door	
cook	floor	
crook		
foot		
forsook		
good		

ü	ō	ŭ
hood		
hoof		
hook		
look		
nook		
rook		
roof		
shook		
soot		
stood		
took		
wood		
woof		
wool		

OUGH – is an unusual phonogram. Many people use this spelling to prove that English is not regular. However, it is possible to think systematically about it. Short /ŏ/ is the most frequent sound. It is found in eight common base words. Long /ō/ is the second most common sound, found in five words; /ö/ is found in one word (for ease of memorization this has been moved to the third position); /ow/ is found in three; /ŭf/ is found in three; /ŏf/ is found in two. Some people also include the sound /ŭp/ as in the old spelling of hiccup: hiccough.

ŏ	ō	ö
bought	though	through
brought	dough	
fought	borough	
nought	furlough	
ought	thorough	
sought		
thought		
wrought		

ow	ŭf	ŏf
bough	enough	cough
drought	rough	trough
plough	tough	

By adding suffixes and prefixes and using these to form compound words, these words can be expanded into a total of 239 words.

U – While it is true that long vowels say their names, the /y/ sound of long /ū/ is often lost after consonants to ease pronunciation. Consider the difference between *cute* and *tune*.

UI – is used in only seven common base words. These may be taught as a group.

bruise	cruise	fruit
juice	nuisance	sluice
suit		

Y – At the end of one-syllable words Y says /ī/. There are 17 words that fit this category:

by	buy	cry	dry
fly	fry	my	ply
pry	shy	sky	sly
spry	sty	try	why
wry			

Y also says /ī/ at the end of multisyllable words, such as *supply, ally,* and *deny,* and with the suffix *-fy.*

At the end of most multisyllable words Y says /ē/. Y is the most common spelling of long /ē/ at the end of multisyllable words.

busy	ugly	berry
candy	mystery	envy

SOUND TO SPELLING REFERENCE

This table represents the common spellings for each sound.

ă	m*a*t	ŭ	*u*p, c*ou*ntry
ā	*a*pron, lat*e*, l*ai*d, pl*ay*, st*ea*k, th*ei*r, th*ey*, *eigh*t	ū	*u*nit, c*u*t*e*, f*ew*
ä	f*a*ther, *au*thor, s*aw*, c*augh*t	ü	p*u*t, t*oo*k, c*ou*ld
b	*b*at, *b*uy	v	*v*an
d	*d*ad, pull*ed*	w	*w*all
ě	*e*lk, br*ea*d	ks	fo*x*
ē	b*e*, *e*v*e*, *ea*t, tr*ee*, prot*ei*n, stad*i*um, k*ey*, p*ie*ce, bab*y*	y	*y*ard, on*i*on
f	*f*at, *ph*one	z	a*s*, *x*ylophone, *z*ip
g	bi*g*, *gu*ide	är	c*ar*
h	*h*at	ch	*ch*ild, but*ch*er
ĭ	*i*t, g*y*m	ěd	trad*ed*
ī	*i*vy, b*y*, n*igh*t, sl*i*d*e*, t*y*p*e*, bl*i*nd, f*ei*sty, h*eigh*t	er	h*er*, b*ir*d, h*ur*t, s*ear*ch
J	e*dge**	ng	si*ng*

* The /j/ sound formed by DGE in words such as *edge* and *fudge* is harsher than the sound heard with the spelling GE as in *large* and *carriage*. Some students will be able to hear the difference for spelling; others will not be able to distinguish DGE as a distinct sound.

j	*j*ob, *g*em, ri*g*id, *g*ym	**oi**	bo*i*l, bo*y*
k	*c*at, *k*it, s*ch*ool, ba*ck*	**ōr**	lo*r*d
l	*l*ap	**ow**	ho*u*se, pl*ow*, b*ough*
m	*m*e	**sh**	*sh*e, *ch*ef, na*ti*on, ses*si*on, spa*ci*ous
n	*n*ut, *gn*at, *kn*ow	**th**	*th*in
ŏ	*o*n, th*ough*t	**TH**	*th*is
ō	g*o*, sm*o*ke, c*o*ld, c*oa*t, t*oe*, fl*oo*r, s*ou*l, sn*ow*, th*ough*	**wer**	*w*o*r*k
ö	t*u*na, d*o*, t*u*ne, f*oo*d, gr*ou*p, fr*ui*t, thr*ough*, fl*ew*, sh*oe*	**wh**	*wh*isper
p	*p*an	**zh**	divi*si*on
kw	*qu*een	**sē**	re*cei*ve
r	*r*an, *wr*ite	**ăf**	la*ugh*
s	*s*ent, *c*ent, *c*ircle, *c*y*c*le	**ŭf**	r*ough*
t	*t*ip, pick*ed*	**ŏf**	tr*ough*
		ə	*o*ther, *a*bout, th*e*

ADVANCED PHONOGRAMS

This table lists the most common advanced phonograms. These phonograms are necessary for learning to read and spell advanced words, but they are not essential to the core vocabulary.

aa	/ä/	n*aa*n			*Dutch, Persian*
ae	/ā-ē-ĕ/	*ae*rial	alg*ae*	*ae*sthetic	*Greek, Latin*
ah	/ä/	helleluj*ah*			*Hebrew*
ai	/ī-ă/	*ai*sle	pl*ai*d		*French, Japanese*
aigh	/ā/	str*aigh*t			*Old English*
au	/ō-ow/	ch*au*vinism	s*au*erkr*au*t		*French, German*
ay	/ī/	c*ay*enne			*French*
bt	/t/	dou*bt*			*Latin*
cc	/k-ch/	sta*cc*ato	ca*pp*u*cc*ino		*Italian*
ce	/sh/	o*ce*an			*Latin*
cu	/k-kw/	bis*cu*it	*cu*isine		*French*
e	/ā/	caf*é*	latt*e*		*French, Italian*
eau	/ō/	plat*eau*			*French*
ée	/ā/	matin*ée*	pur*ee*		*French*
ei	/ī-ĕ/	forf*ei*t	h*ei*fer		*Middle English*
eo	/ē-ĕ/	p*eo*ple	l*eo*pard		*Middle English*
et	/ā/	gourm*et*			*French*
eu	/ö-ū/	n*eu*tral	f*eu*d		*Latin, Mid English*

eur	/yer-er/	*Eur*ope	chauff*eur*	*French*
ge	/j-ZH/	sur*ge*on	camoufla*ge*	*French*
gh	/g/	*gh*astly		*Old English, Italian*
gi	/j/	re*gi*on		*French, Latin*
gn	/ny/	poi*gn*ant		*French, Italian*
ie	/ĕ/	fr*ie*nd		*Old English*
j	/h-y/	*j*alapeno	*fj*ord	*Spanish, Norwegian*
kh	/k/	*kh*aki		*Persian*
mb	/m/	bo*mb*		*Old English*
mn	/m-n/	hy*mn*	*mn*emonic	*Greek, Latin*
oe	/ē/	subp*oe*na		*Latin*
oi	/wä/	mem*oi*r		*French*
ot	/ō/	dep*ot*		*French*
our	/er/	j*our*ney		*French, English*
pn	/n/	*pn*eumonia		*Greek*
ps	/s/	*p*sychology		*Greek*
pt	/t/	*pt*erodactyl		*Greek*
qu	/k/	criti*qu*e		*Spanish, French*
rh	/r/	*rh*ythm		*Greek*
s	silent	debri*s*		*French*
sc	/s-sh/	*sc*ene	cre*sc*endo	*Latin*
sch	/sh/	*sch*wa		*German*
sci	/sh/	con*sci*ence		*Latin*
th	/t/	*th*yme		*Middle English*
ut	/ū/	deb*ut*		*French*
xi	/ksh/	an*xi*ous		*Latin*
yr	/er/	m*yr*tle		*Greek*
z	/s/	quart*z*		*German*

ADDING A SUFFIX TO ANY WORD

Does it end with a **Silent Final E**?
Does it end with **One Vowel + One Consonant** (seen and heard)?
Does it end with a **Y**?

> If **yes,** continue with the questions for the word type below.
> If **no**, just add the suffix.

Silent Final E

Are we adding a vowel suffix?
Is dropping the E allowed by other spelling rules?

> C says /s/ before E, I, and Y.
> G may say /j/ before E, I, and Y.
> If **yes**, drop the E and add the suffix.
> If **no**, just add the suffix.

One Vowel + One Consonant

Are we adding a vowel suffix?
Is the syllable before the suffix stressed?

> If **yes**, double the last consonant and add the suffix.
> If **no**, just add the suffix.

Single Vowel Y

Does it end with a single vowel Y?
Does the suffix begin with any letter except I?

> If **yes**, change the Y to I and add the suffix.
> If **no**, retain the Y and add the ending.

IRREGULAR VERBS

This list of 168 irregular verbs only includes base words. Many of these words form derivatives.

Present	Simple Past	Past Participle
be (am, is, are)	was (were)	been
bear	bore	born/borne
beat	beat	beaten/beat
become	became	become
begin	began	begun
bend	bent	bent
bereave	bereaved/bereft	bereaved/bereft
bet	bet	bet
bid (on a price. Ex. auctions)	bid	bid
bid (to request)	bade/bid	bidden/bid
bind	bound	bound
bite	bit	bitten
bleed	bled	bled
blow	blew	blown
break	broke	broken
breed	bred	bred
bring	brought	brought
build	built	built
burn	burned/burnt	burned/burnt
burst	burst/bursted	burst/bursted
buy	bought	bought

Present	Simple Past	Past Participle
can	could	could
cast	cast	cast
catch	caught	caught
choose	chose	chosen
cleave (split apart)	clove	cloven
cleave (cling to)	cleft/cleaved	cleft/cleaved
cling	clung	clung
come	came	come
cost	cost	cost
creep	crept	crept
cut	cut	cut
deal	dealt	dealt
dig	dug	dug
dive	dove	dived
do	did	done
drag	drug/dragged	drug/dragged
draw	drew	drawn
dream	dreamt/dreamed	dreamt/dreamed
drink	drank/drunk	drunk/drunken
drive	drove	driven
dwell	dwelt/dwelled	dwelt/dwelled
eat	ate	eaten
fall	fell	fallen
feed	fed	fed
feel	felt	felt
fight	fought	fought
find	found	found
fit	fit/fitted	fit/fitted
flee	fled	fled
fling	flung	flung
fly	flew	flown

Present	Simple Past	Past Participle
freeze	froze	frozen
fret	fret/fretted	fret/fretted
get	got	gotten/got
give	gave	given
go	went	gone
grind	ground	ground
grow	grew	grown
hang	hung/hanged	hung/hanged
have	had	had
hear	heard	heard
hew	hew/hewed	hewn
hide	hid	hid/hidden
hit	hit	hit
hold	held	held
hurt	hurt	hurt
keep	kept	kept
kneel	knelt/kneeled	knelt/kneeled
knit	knit/knitted	knit/knitted
know	knew	known
lay	laid	laid
lead	led	led
leap	leaped/leapt	leaped/leapt
leave	left	left
lend	lent	lent
let	let	let
lie	lay	lain
light	lit/lighted	lit/lighted
lose	lost	lost
make	made	made
may	might	
mean	meant	meant
meet	met	met

Present	Simple Past	Past Participle
mow	mowed	mowed/mown
pay	paid	paid
put	put	put
quit	quit	quit
read	read	read
rend	rent	rent
rid	rid/ridded	rid/ridden/ridded
ride	rode	ridden
ring	rang	rung
rise	rose	risen
run	ran	run
saw	sawed	sawed/sawn
say	said	said
see	saw	seen
seek	sought	sought
sell	sold	sold
send	sent	sent
set	set	set
sew	sewed	sewed/sewn
shake	shook	shaken
shall	should	
shave	shaved	shaven/shaved
shear	sheared	shorn/sheared
shed	shed	shed
shoe	shoed/shod	shoed/shod
shoot	shot	shot
show	showed	shown
shrink	shrank/shrunk	shrunk/shrunken
shut	shut	shut
sing	sang	sung
sink	sank/sunk	sunk/sunken

Present	Simple Past	Past Participle
sit	sat	sat
slay	slew	slain
sleep	slept	slept
slide	slid	slid
sling	slang/slung	slung
slink	slunk/slinked	slunk/slinked
slit	slit	slit
smite	smote	smitten
sneak	sneaked/snuck	sneaked/snuck
sow	sowed	sowed/sown
speak	spoke	spoken
speed	sped/speeded	sped/speeded
spend	spent	spent
spin	spun	spun
spit	spit/spat	spit
split	split	split
spoil	spoiled/spoilt	spoiled/spoilt
spread	spread	spread
spring	sprang/sprung	sprung
stand	stood	stood
steal	stole	stolen
stick	stuck	stuck
sting	stung	stung
stink	stank/stunk	stunk
strew	strew/strewed	strewn/strewed
stride	strode	stridden
strike	struck	stricken/struck
string	strung	strung
strive	strove/strived	striven/strived
swear	swore	sworn
sweep	swept	swept

Present	Simple Past	Past Participle
swell	swelled	swelled/swollen
swim	swam	swum
swing	swung	swung
take	took	taken
teach	taught	taught
tear	tore	torn
tell	told	told
think	thought	thought
throw	threw	thrown
thrust	thrust	thrust
tread	trod	trodden/trod
wake	woke	woken
wear	wore	worn
weave	wove	woven
wed	wed	wed
weep	wept	wept
wet	wet	wet
will	would	willed
win	won	won
wind	wound	wound
wring	wrung	wrung
write	wrote	written

IRREGULAR PLURALS

The root of each form is noted: OE Old English, F French, H Hebrew, I Italian, G Greek and L Latin.

Root	Changes	Singular	Plural	Normalized to English Spelling
OE	→ en	child	children	
		man	men	
		ox	oxen	
		woman	women	
OE	oo → ee	foot	feet	
		goose	geese	
		tooth	teeth	
OE	ouse → ice	louse	lice	
		mouse	mice	
F	eau → eaux	beau	beaux	
		bureau	bureaux	bureaus
		chateau	chateaux	chateaus
G	→ ta	schema	schemata	
H	→ bim	cherub	cherubim	cherubs
		seraph	seraphim	seraphs
		kibbutz	kibbutzim	kibbutzes
I	o → i	tempo	tempi	tempos
		virtuoso	virtuosi	virtuosos
L	a → ae	antenna	antennae	antennas
		formula	formulae	formulas

Root	Changes	Singular	Plural	Normalized to English Spelling
	a → ae (cont'd)	larva	larvae	
		nebula	nebulae	nebulas
		vertebra	vertebrae	
L	is → es	analysis	analyses	
		axis	axes	
		basis	bases	
		crisis	crises	
		diagnosis	diagnoses	
		ellipsis	ellipses	
		emphasis	emphases	
		hypothesis	hypotheses	
		neurosis	neuroses	
		oasis	oases	
		parenthesis	parentheses	
		synopsis	synopses	
		thesis	theses	
L	ex/ix → ices	apex	apices	apexes
		appendix	appendices	appendixes
		index	indices	indexes
		matrix	matrices	matrixes
		vertex	vertices	
L	um/on → a	addendum	addenda	
		bacterium	bacteria	
		criterion	criteria	
		curriculum	curricula	curriculums
		datum	data	
		erratum	errata	
		medium	media	mediums
		millennium	millennia	
		memorandum	memoranda	memorandums
		phenomenon	phenomena	phenomenons

Root	Changes	Singular	Plural	Normalized to English Spelling
	um/on → a	stratum	strata	
	(cont'd)	symposium	symposia	symposiums
L	us → i	alumnus	alumni	alums
		bacillus	bacilli	
		cactus	cacti	cactuses
		focus	foci	focuses
		fungus	fungi	funguses
		nucleus	nuclei	
		octopus	octopi	octopuses
		radius	radii	
		stimulus	stimuli	
		syllabus	syllabi	syllabuses

COMMON PREFIXES AND SUFFIXES

20 Common Prefixes

Prefix	Meaning	Example words
un-	not, opposite	undo, unhappy, unimportant
re-	again, back	redo, remix, return
in-, im-, ir- il-	not, opposite	invisible, imperfect, irresponsible, illiterate
dis-	not, opposite	dislike, distaste, disloyal
en-, em-	to make, to put into, to cause	enact, encourage, encircle, employ
non-	not, opposite	nonthreatening, nonfiction, nonstop
in-, im-	within, in, into	inside, insight, invest
over-	much more than, too much	overdo, overstate, overload, overheat
mis-	bad, wrong, not	misunderstand, misplace
sub-	under, below	subconscious, substandard
pre-	before	predawn, preset, preview
inter-	between, among	intermix, intermingle, intertwine
fore-	before	foretaste, foreclose, forehand
de-	take away	defrost, deforest, deflate
trans-	across, through	transmit, transfusion, transport
super-	over, high, big, extreme	superhighway, superhuman
semi-	half, part	semicircle, semiconductor
anti-	against	antidepressant, antifreeze
mid-	middle	midday, midsummer, midnight
under-	low, too little	underfed, underweight

20 Common Suffixes

Suffix	Meaning	Example Words
-s, -es	*Plural*	chairs, boxes
-ed	*Past tense/past participle*	walked, climbed
-ing	*Gerund/present participle*	walking, climbing
-ly	*Adverbs*	lively, quickly
-er, -or	*Nouns* person or thing that does something	climber, actor
-ion, -tion, -ation, -ition	*Nouns* that denote action or condition	action, creation
-ible, -able	*Adjectives*, having the quality of	forcible, comfortable
-al, -ial	*Noun* act or process of	refusal, proposal
-y	*Adjectives* characterized by	runny, honesty
-ness	*Noun* state of being	laziness, heaviness
-ity, -ty	*Noun* quality of	ability, community
-ment	*Noun* condition of	contentment, commitment
-ic, ical	*Adjective* pertaining to	angelic, tyrannical
-ous, -eous,	*Adjective* full of	autonomous, spontaneous
-en	*Verb* to become	tighten, lighten
-er	*Comparative*	happier, madder
-ive, -ative, -itive	*Adjective* tendency, function	destructive, supportive
-ful	*Adjective* full (of), characterized by	glassful, beautiful
-less	*Adjective* without, free of	hopeless, guiltless
-est	*Superlative*	happiest, fullest

AMERICAN, BRITISH, CANADIAN, AND AUSTRALIAN SPELLINGS

Though there is an amazing conformity among spellings in different regions of the English speaking world, there are a few differences. Many of these differences can be credited to Noah Webster. In 1828, following the American Revolution, Webster set himself to writing the first American Dictionary. In order to distinguish the newly founded country from the country from which they had just won independence, Webster modified some of the spellings to create an "American" version of English. As you will observe in the lists below, some of Webster's changes generated exceptions and inconsistencies that do not exist in the British spellings and some of his changes resolved exceptions. Commonwealth countries typically follow British spelling conventions. Canadian English, however, reflects its history as a Commonwealth as well as a close neighbor of the United States. Sometimes both spellings are acceptable. In this case the most common spelling will be referenced first.

The following dictionaries were referenced for creating these tables:

Delbridge, Arthur. 1981. The Macquarie Dictionary. Concise Digital Edition. St. Leonards, N.S.W.: Macquarie Library.

Merriam-Webster's Collegiate Dictionary. 1993. Springfield, Mass.: Merriam-Webster. Web.

De Wolf, Gaelan Dodds. 1996. Gage Canadian Dictionary. Vancouver: Gage Educational Publishing, Canada.

DG & DGE

The American spelling is an exception to Logic of English spelling rules. DGE is a phonogram and therefore the E should not be dropped when adding a suffix. Even if it were a silent final E, the rule states to drop the E only before a vowel suffix. In these words the Australian, British, and Canadian spellings follow the rules more closely.

American	Australian	British	Canadian
acknowle*dg*ment	acknowle*dge*ment	acknowle*dge*ment	acknowle*dge*ment
ju*dg*ment	ju*dge*ment	ju*dge*ment	ju*dge*ment

S & Z

American spellings frequently use the phonogram Z where British and Australian spellings use the second sound of S. Canadian spellings of these words reflect both the American and British conventions.

American	Australian	British	Canadian
amortize	amortise	amortise	amortize
analyze	analyse	analyse	analyse
apologize	apologise	apologise	apologize
authorize	authorise	authorise	authorize
capitalize	capitalise	capitalise	capitalize
catalyze	catalyse	catalyse	
cozy	cosy	cosy	cozy
criticize	criticise	criticise	criticize
emphasize	emphasise	emphasise	emphasize
galvanize	galvanise	galvanise	galvanize
generalize	generalise	generalise	generalize
initialize		initialise	initialize
optimize	optimise	optimise	optimize
organization	organisation	organisation	organization

organize	organise	organise	organize
paralyze	paralyse	paralyse	paralyze
realize	realise	realise	realize
recognize	recognise	recognise	recognize
standardize	standardise	standardise	standardize

C & S

Occasionally American spellings use the phonogram S followed by a silent final E with Rule 12.5. The British and Australian spellings use a C followed by a silent final E, Rule 12.3.

American	Australian	British	Canadian
defense	defence	defence	
offense	offence	offence	
pretense	pretence	pretence	

G & GU

American spellings use the simple phonogram G. British and Canadian spellings use the phonogram GU. Since English words cannot end in U, a silent final E is added.

American	Australian	British	Canadian
analog	analog	analogue	analogue
catalog	catalogue	catalogue	catalogue
dialog	dialogue	dialogue	dialogue

OR & OUR

Many American spellings use the phonogram OR where Australian, British, and Canadian spellings use OUR. For this reason, students in the UK and Canada should add the Advanced Phonogram OUR to the Basic Phonograms. In addition, British spellings occasionally drop the U when adding a Latin based suffix, thereby spelling derivatives such as *honorary, vigorous, humorous, laborious,* and *invigorate* without the phonogram OUR. Wherever the vowel is clearly pronounced, the words are spelled the same throughout the English-speaking world: *contour* and *velour.*

American	Australian	British	Canadian
armor	armour	armour	armour
behavior	behaviour	behaviour	behaviour
candor	candour	candour	candour
clamor	clamour	clamour	clamour
color	colour	colour	colour
demeanor	demeanour	demeanour	demeanour
endeavor	endeavour	endeavour	endeavour
favor	favour	favour	favour
favorite	favourite	favourite	favourite
flavor	flavour	flavour	flavour
harbor	harbour	harbour	harbour
honor	honour	honour	honour
humor	humour	humour	humour
labor	labour	labour	labour
neighbor	neighbour	neighbour	neighbour
odor	odour	odour	odor
parlor	parlour	parlour	parlour
rigor	rigour	rigour	rigour
rumor	rumour	rumour	rumour
tumor	tumour	tumour	tumour
vapor	vapour	vapour	vapour

CK & QUE

Some American and Australian spellings use the phonogram CK where British and Canadian spellings use the phonogram QU followed by a silent final E.

American	Australian	British	Canadian
check	check	cheque	cheque
checkered	checkered	chequered	chequered

ER & RE

Some British spellings utilize R followed by a silent final E for words where the American convention is to use the phonogram ER. Australian and Canadian spellings typically follow the British. In the British convention the silent final E is providing a written vowel for the syllable. Noah Webster, however, forgot one word when changing this convention for Americans. *Acre* still follows the British convention for spelling. In addition, many British spellings use the ER phonogram as in *chapter, disaster, filter, letter, member, number, October, powder, paper...*

American	Australian	British	Canadian
caliber	calibre	calibre	calibre
center	centre	centre	centre
fiber	fibre	fibre	fibre
liter	litre	litre	
luster	lustre	lustre	
meager	meagre	meagre	meagre
meter	metre	metre	metre
saber	sabre	sabre	
somber	sombre	sombre	
theater	theatre	theatre	

Double Consonants

British and American spellings follow the rule: "Double the last consonant when adding a vowel suffix to words ending in one vowel followed by one consonant, only if the syllable before the suffix is stressed." However, for British spellings,

L's are doubled regardless of which syllable is stressed. In the United States it is common not to double the L in an unstressed syllable; however, both spellings are listed as acceptable in Merriam Webster's Dictionary. Unfortunately, Canadians will need to memorize the exceptions word by word since their spelling has been influenced by both the British and American spellings.

Though only one derivative is included for each of the base words, the rules apply to all derivatives formed from the base. For example: *counselled, counselling, counsellor…*

American	Australian	British	Canadian
canceled/cancelled	cancelled	cancelled	cancelled
counselor/ counsellor	counsellor	counsellor	counsellor
dialing/dialling	dialling	dialling	dialing
fueling/fuelling	fuelling	fuelling	fuelling
installment/ instalment	instalment	instalment	instalment
jewelry	jewellery	jewellery	jewellery
labeled/labelled	labelled	labelled	labelled
marvelous/ marvellous	marvellous	marvellous	marvellous
modeled/modelled	modelled	modelled	modelled
signaling signalling	signalling	signalling	signalling
snorkeling	snorkelling	snorkelling	snorkelling
woolen	woollen	woollen	woollen

Roots

Occasionally American and British spellings will originate from different roots with the same meaning. For example: *airplane* and *aeroplane*. (AE is an advanced phonogram.)

American	Australian	British	Canadian
*air*plane	*aero*plane	*aero*plane	*air*plane

Added Syllables

A few words are pronounced with an additional syllable in British English compared to American English, which is then reflected in the spelling.

American	Australian	British	Canadian
aluminum	alumin*i*um	alumin*i*um	aluminum
specialty	specialty	special*i*ty	specialty

T & ED

Some verbs which are treated as regular verbs in American English are treated as irregular verbs with British spelling conventions. Where the American spelling uses ED to represent the past tense, British spelling uses the irregular verb form spelled with a single-letter T.

American	Australian	British	Canadian
dream*ed*/dream*t*	dream*ed*/dream*t*	dream*t*	
learn*ed*	learn*t*	learn*t*	

AE & E

Where some American spellings use the single-letter phonogram E, British spellings use the phonogram AE. Notice all of these words are derived from Latin roots. Two words retain the AE spelling in American English: *aesthetics* and *archaeology*.

American	Australian	British	Canadian
an*e*sthesia	an*ae*sthesia	an*ae*sthesia	
an*e*mia	an*ae*mia	an*ae*mia	

encyclopedia	encyclopedia	encyclopaedia
gynecology	gynecology	gynaecology
leukemia	leukaemia	leukaemia
medieval	mediaeval	mediaeval
orthopedic		orthopaedic
paleontology	palaeontology	palaeontology
pediatric		paediatric

OE & E

Where some American spellings use the single-letter phonogram E, Australian and British spellings use the phonogram OE. Notice all of these words are derived from Latin roots.

American	Australian	British	Canadian
diarrhea	diarrhoea	diarrhoea	
maneuver	manoeuvre	manoeuvre	

Other

Occasionally words also vary by one phonogram.

American	Australian	British	Canadian
artifact	artefact	artefact	artifact
pajamas	pyjamas	pyjamas	pyjamas
gray	grey	grey	grey
mold	mould	mould	mould

RESOURCES

Resources for Teaching

Logic of English Essentials Curriculum—Forty step-by-step lessons for teaching the phonograms, spelling rules, reading, grammar, and sentence level writing to students of all ages.

Logic of English Foundations Curriculum—Step-by-step lessons for teaching the phonograms, spelling rules, reading, and handwriting to young, beginning students (ages 4-7).

Phonogram Flashcards—74 Basic Phonogram Cards.

Spelling Rule Flashcards—Flashcards for practicing the 31 spelling rules.

Advanced Phonogram Flashcards—Flashcards for practicing the advanced phonograms.

Questions and Professional Development

Logic of English Forums—a place to discuss the phonograms, the rules, and their role in learning and teaching English. Available at www.LogicofEnglish. com/forum.

Logic of English YouTube Videos—Watch our ever growing collection of videos on the Logic of English YouTube channel. http://www.youtube.com/ user/LogicofEnglish?feature=watch

Websites Related to The Logic of English

www.LogicofEnglish.com
Includes additional products, webstore, forums for discussion, English language blog, and more.

www.DeniseEide.com
Author's website including speaking schedule and blog.

OTHER WEBSITES

www.dictionary.reference.com
Online dictionary.

www.nationalreadingpanel.org
Findings of the National Reading Panel. These findings support the use of systematic phonics in the classroom.

www.morewords.com
Useful for investigating phonograms.

www.findtheword.info
Useful for investigating phonograms.

www.krysstal.com
Words borrowed from other languages.

http://nces.ed.gov/nationsreportcard/
Current U.S. statistics on the literacy crisis.

www.lewrockwell.com/snyder-joshua/snyder-joshua9.html
Article on the history of English spelling and why it should not be changed.

GLOSSARY

advanced phonogram—phonograms necessary for learning to read and spell advanced words, but not essential to the core vocabulary. For a list of advanced phonograms, see Appendix E.

affix—a group of letters added to either the beginning or ending of a word. There are two types of affixes in English: suffixes and prefixes.

base word—a word that can stand alone when all the affixes have been removed. Let's consider the word *renew*. If we remove the prefix *re-*, the base word *new* is left. *New* is a recognizable English word that stands alone, therefore it is a base word.

consonant—a sound which is blocked by the tongue, teeth, or lips in some way. Most consonants are difficult to sing or control for volume. The single consonants are: b, c, d, f, g, h, j, k, l, m, n, p, qu, r, s, t, v, w, x, (y), z.

consonant suffix—begins with a consonant such as *-ly, -ness, -ful, -hood,* and *-ment*.

derivative—a word formed by adding suffixes and prefixes to a root or by combining two base words to form a compound word.

morpheme—the smallest word part that carries meaning. Morphemes include roots, base words, suffixes, and prefixes. For example the word *dogs* consists of two morphemes: the base word, *dog,* and the suffix, *-s*.

multi-letter phonogram—a phonogram which is written with two or more letters.

phonogram—a letter or combination of letters which represents one or more sounds.

prefix—a group of letters added to the beginning of a root that alters the meaning.

root—carries the primary meaning of the word but is not necessarily an English word when all the affixes have been removed. For example, *move* is the root of the word *remove*. *Move* stands alone so it is also a base word. The word *revive* also has the prefix re-. However, the root *vive* is not a base word because it is not a recognizable English word. *Vive* is a root, but not a base word.

schwa /ə/—an unstressed vowel which sounds very similar to short /ŭ/.

silent final E—an E at the end of a base word that is not sounded. There are nine types of silent final E's.

single-letter phonogram—a phonogram written with only one letter. They are represented by the letters A–Z.

single vowel Y—a Y that is acting alone at the end of the word; it is not part of one of the multi-letter phonograms ay, ey, or oy.

stressed syllable—the one that is said a bit louder or stronger than the others.

suffix—a group of letters added to the end of a root which alters the meaning or part of speech.

syllable—a rhythmic part of a word produced when the mouth opens to form a vowel sound.

vowel—a sound that is produced when the mouth is open and the sound is not blocked by the lips, teeth, or tongue. Vowels are sounds that can be sustained such as in singing and controlled for volume.

vowel suffix—an ending that begins with a vowel. For example: *-able, -ing, -ed, -ish,* and *-y.*

BIBLIOGRAPHY

Alliance for Excellent Education. 2006. *Paying Double: Inadequate High Schools and Community College Remediation.* www.all4ed.org/publication_material/PayingDouble.

American Psychological Association. 2006. *See Brain. See Brain Read.* www. readingrockets.org/article/30205.

The Annie E. Casey Foundation. 2009. "4th Grade Reading Achievement Levels." *KIDS COUNT Data Center.* http://datacenter.kidscount.org/data/acrossstates/Rankings .aspx?ind=5116.

———. *2009.* "4th Grade Reading Achievement Levels (Percent)." *KIDS COUNT Data Center.* http://datacenter.kidscount.org/data/acrossstates/Rankings.aspx?ind=5116.

Begin to Read. n.d. *Literacy Statistics.* www.begintoread.com/research/ literacystatistics.html.

Bishop, Margaret M. 1986. The ABC's and All Their Tricks. Fenton, MI: Mott Media.

Bumgardner, Brooke. 2007. *The Role Literacy Plays in Crime.* http://www.associatedcontent .com/article/273893/the_role_literacy_plays_in_crime_pg8.html?cat=17.

Clecker, Bob C. 2008. *Let's End Our Literacy Crisis* revised edition. Salt Lake City, UT: American University and College Press.

Cook, Gina. 2011. *Grapheme Cards.* Linguist-Educator Exchange.

Flesch, Rudolf. 1955. *Why Johnny Can't Read and What You Can Do About It.* New York: Harper.

Fletcher, Jack M, PhD. *What's Happening in the Reading Brain.* www.texasreading.org /downloads/trfi/principals_retreat/1.4JfletcherPresentation.pdf.

Green, Tamara M. 2008. *The Greek and Latin Roots of English.* Plymouth, UK: Rowman and Littlefield Publishers, Inc.

Kieffer, Michael J. and Lesaux, Nonie K. 2007. "Breaking Down Words to Build Meaning." In William F. Graves, ed. 2009. *Essential Readings on Vocabulary Instruction.* Newark, DE.

Literacy Texas. n.d. Literacy Facts. www.literacytexas.org/index.php/resources /literacy_facts/.

McGuinness, Diane. 1997. *Why Our Children Can't Read: And What We Can Do About It.* New York, New York: Touchstone.

———. 2004. *Early Reading Instruction: What Science Really Teaches Us about How to Teach Reading.* Cambridge, MA: Bradford Books.

Myers, Bob. Dec 21, 2008. *10 Years of Brain Imaging Research Shows the Brain Reads Sound by Sound.* www.healthyplace.com/adhd/add-focus/10-years-of-brain -imaging-research-shows-the-brain-reads-sound-by-sound/menu-id-1580/.

National Center for Education Statistics. 2011. *The Nation's Report Card.* *http://nces.ed.gov/pubsearch/pubsinfo.asp?pubid=2012457.*

National Institute of Child Health and Human Development. 2000. *Report of the National Reading Panel. Teaching Children to Read: An Evidence-Based Assessment of the Scientific Research Literature on Reading and its Implications for Reading Instruction.* http://www.nichd.nih.gov/publications/nrp/smallbook.htm.

Nyikos, Julius. 1988. "A Linguistic Perspective of Functional Illiteracy." *The Fourteenth LACUS Forum 1987.* Lake Bluff, IL: Linguistic Association of Canada and the United States.

Rasinski, Timothy, Nancy Padak, Rick M. Newton, and Evangeline Newton. 2010. *Greek & Latin Roots: Keys to Building Vocabulary.* Huntington Beach, CA: Shell Education.

Sanseri, Wanda. 2009. *Spell to Write and Read.* Milwaukie, OR: Back Home Industries, Inc.

Shaywitz, Sally E. November 1996. "Dyslexia." *Scientific American* 275(5)(Nove.):63–69.

Smart Future. n.d. http://arkansased.org/smart_future.html.

Spalding, Romalda. 1990. *The Writing Road to Reading* fourth revised edition. New York: Quill William Morrow.

White, Sowell and Yangihara. 1989. "Teaching Elementary Students to use Word-Part Clues." *Essential Readings on Vocabulary Instruction.*

NOTES

Introduction

1 National Center for Education Statistics. 2011. *The Nation's Report Card* . http://nces.ed.gov/pubsearch/pubsinfo.asp?pubid=2012457.

2 Ibid., 26.

3 McGuinness, Diane. 1997. *Why Our Children Can't Read: And What We Can Do About It* . New York, New York: Touchstone. 10.

4 Literacy Texas. n.d. Literacy Facts. www.literacytexas.org/index.php/resources/ literacy_facts/.

5 Bumgardner, Brooke. 2007. *The Role Literacy Plays in Crime.* www.associatedcontent.com /article/273893/the_role_literacy_plays_in_crime_pg8.html?cat=17.

6 McGuinness. *Why Our Children Can't Read,* 12.

Chapter 1

1 Nyikos, Julius. 1988. "A Linguistic Perspective of Functional Illiteracy." *The Fourteenth LACUS Forum 1987.* Lake Bluff, IL: Linguistic Association of Canada and the United States, 146-163

2 Rasinski, Timothy, Nancy Padak, Rick M. Newton, and Evangeline Newton. 2010 *Greek & Latin Roots: Keys to Building Vocabulary.* Huntington Beach, CA: Shell Education, 11.

3 Ibid.

4 McGuinness, Diane. 2004. *Early Reading Instruction: What Science Really Teaches Us about How to Teach Reading.* Cambridge, MA: Bradford Books, 5.

5 McGuinness. *Why our Children Can't Read,* 45.

6 McGuinness. *Early Reading Instruction.*

Chapter 2

1 The Annie E. Casey Foundation. 2009. "4th Grade Reading Achievement Levels." *KIDS COUNT Data Center.* http://datacenter.kidscount.org/data/acrossstates/Rankings.aspx?ind=5116.

2 National Center for Education Statistics. 2009. *The Nation's Report Card.* http://nationsreportcard .gov/reading_2009/reading_2009_tudareport/, 26.

3 Ibid.

4 McGuinness. *Why our Children Can't Read,* 10.

5 Ibid.

6 Ibid.

7 Smart Future. n.d. http://arkansased.org/smart_future.html.

8 McGuinness. *Why our Children Can't Read,* 10.

9 Literacy Texas. n.d. Literacy Facts. www.literacytexas.org/index.php/resources/ literacy_facts/.

10 Ibid.

11 Alliance for Excellent Education. 2006. *Paying Double: Inadequate High Schools and Community College Remediation.* www.all4ed.org/publication_material/PayingDouble.

12 Literacy Texas.

13 Alliance for Excellent Education.

14 Alliance for Excellent Education.

15 Flesch, Rudolf. 1955. *Why Johnny Can't Read and What You Can Do About It.* New York: Harper.

16 National Center for Education Statistics.

17 Clecker, Bob C. 2008. *Let's End Our Literacy Crisis* revised edition. Salt Lake City, UT: American University and College Press, 61.

18 McGuinness. *Why our Children Can't Read, 10.*

19 American Psychological Association 2006. *See Brain. See Brain Read.* www. readingrockets.org /article/30205.

Chapter 3

1   Myers, Bob. Dec 21, 2008. *10 Years of Brain Imaging Research Shows the Brain Reads Sound by Sound.* www.healthyplace.com/adhd/add-focus/10-years-of-brain-imaging-research-shows-the -brain-reads-sound-by-sound/menu-id-1580/.

2   Ibid.

Chapter 5

1   www.morewords.com: 4,000 examples for *ce*, more than 4,000 for *ci*, and 1,124 containing *cy*.

Chapter 6

1   These words were identified using www.morewords.com.

Chapter 7

1   American Psychological Association.

2   Myers. *10 Years of Brain Imaging Research Shows the Brain Reads Sound by Sound.*

3   McGuinness. *Why our Children Can't Read, 45.*

Chapter 9

1   Wikipedia. November 2010. "Commonly Misspelled Words." Retrieved from: http://en.wikipedia.org /wiki/commonly_misspelled_words.

Chapter 11

1   Bishop, Margaret M. 1986. *The ABC's and All Their Tricks.* Fenton, MI: Mott Media, 95.

2   Ibid, 96.

3   Ibid, 97.

Chapter 12

1   World Lingo. "Multilingual Archive: irregular verbs." www.worldlingo.com/ma/ enwiki/en /irregular_verb.

Chapter 16

1   McGuinness. *Early Reading Instruction, 40.*

In 1973 researchers tested 240 Finnish children in grades 1–3. They were given a nonsense word reading test which included all of the possible spelling combinations in Finnish. At the end of first grade, children averaged a score of 80% accuracy. College students scored 90% on the same test.

Chapter 17

1   Kieffer, Michael J. and Lesaux, Nonie K. 2007. "Breaking Down Words to Build Meaning." In William F. Graves, ed. 2009. *Essential Readings on Vocabulary Instruction.* Newark, DE. *92.*

2   White, Sowell and Yangihara. 1989. "Teaching Elementary Students to use Word-Part Clues." *Essential Readings on Vocabulary Instruction, 84.*

3   Ibid.

4   Green, Tamara M. 2008. *The Greek and Latin Roots of English.* Plymouth, UK: Rowman and Littlefield Publishers, Inc, xi.

5   Rasinski, Timothy, Nancy Padak, Rick M. Newton, and Evangeline Newton. 2010. *Greek & Latin Roots: Keys to Building Vocabulary.* Huntington Beach, CA: Shell Education, 11.

SUBJECT INDEX

accent, 78-85

adding suffixes to
    1 consonant + 1 vowel words, 77-86
    any word, 92, 171
    silent final E words, 71-76
    single vowel Y words, 87-90

affix, *130*, 135, *195*

base word, *130*, *195*

compound words, 114, 132
consonant, *37*, *195*
count nouns, 109

derivatives, *130*, *195*
dialects, 122-124

English words that end in I, 47, 51-53
exceptions, 45, 54-56, 61, 74-76, 85-86,
       89-90, 100, 103

Greek roots, 135-139

high frequency words, 129-*130*

I, English words that end in, 47, 51-53
irregular
    nouns, 107, 110
    plurals, 179-181
    verbs, 104-106, 111-112, 173-178

Latin roots, 97-98
Latin spellings of SH, 95-100
literacy crisis, 21-24
logical/literal students, 27

long sound, vowel says its name
    before a silent final E, 64
    at the end of the syllable, 56-57

multi-letter phonogram aids, 34-35
morpheme *130*, *195*

nouns
    irregular, 107, 110, 179-181
    non-count, 109

past tense, 101-106
phoneme, *15*, 16, 24
phonogram
    advanced, 31, *195*, 169-170
    aids for spelling, 31, 34-35
    basic 153-155, 157-168
    definition, *16*, *25*, *195*
    multi-letter, 28, 30, 32-35, *195*
    multi-letter spelling aids, 31, 34-35
    single-letter, 26-29, *196*
plurals, 68-69, 107-110
prefix, 113-114, *130*, 132-133, 183, *196*

QU 61, 81

roots, *130*, 135-139, *195*
rules. *see* spelling rules

Say to Spell, 125-127
schwa, 79, *124*, 196
spelling rules by number
    complete list, 151-152
    Rule 1, *43*, 42-45
    Rule 2, *46*, 45-47

Rule 3, *47*, 51-56

Rule 4, *56* , 57

Rule 5, *57*

Rule 6, *58*

Rule 7, *58-59*

Rule 8, 59

Rule 9, *59*

Rule 10, *60*

Rule 11, *61*

Rule 12.1, *64*

Rule 12.2, *66*, 65-66

Rule 12.3, *67*, 66-67

Rule 12.4, *67*

Rule 12.5, *68*, 69

Rule 12.6, *69*

Rule 12.7, *70*

Rule 12.8, *70*

Rule 12.9, *71*

Rule 13, *71*, 72-74

Rule 14, *80*, 79-86

Rule 15, *88*, 89

Rule 16, *89*

Rule 17, *98*

Rule 18, *99*, 100

Rule 19, *101*, 102-103

Rule 20, *103*

Rule 21, *107*, 108-110

Rule 22, *111*, 110-112

Rule 23, *113*, 114

Rule 24, *113*, 114

Rule 25, *115*, 116

Rule 26, *116*

Rule 27, *116*

Rule 28, *117*

Rule 29, *117*, 118

Rule 30, *118*, 119

schwa, 124

suffix, 71, 77, 113-114, *130*, 133-134, 184, *196*

    added to silent final E words, 71-75

    1 consonant + 1 vowel words, 77-86

    consonant suffix, 72, 82, *195*

    single vowel Y words, 87-90

    vowel suffix, 71-72, 80, *196*

syllables, 38-39, 67, *196*

tense

    past, 101-106

    present, 111-112

third person singular verbs, 110-112

verbs, irregular, 101, 104-106, 111-112,

      173-178

vocabulary development, 129-139

vowel, *37*, 37-39, 41, 49-61, 64-66, 67-76, *196*

vowel says its long sound

    at the end of a syllable, 56-57

    before a silent final E, 64

ABOUT THE AUTHOR

 Denise Eide is an educator, author, speaker, and curriculum designer. She has worked in the field of literacy instruction since 1995. Her specialty is teaching reading and spelling to educators and parents by helping them understand the logic of English and demonstrating teaching methods that ensure success for students of all learning styles. Her desire is for these methods to be available to all students, parents, and educators, leading to a dramatic reversal in America's literacy crisis. She lives in Rochester, Minnesota, with her husband and four children.